Travels in Ireland
Johann Georg Kohl

I0145614

Part 4

A Clachan Reprint

Clachan Publishing,

Ballycastle : Northern Ireland, 2016

Travels in Ireland:
Johann Georg Kohl

Part 4
Chapters 30-39
By J. G. Kohl
Translated from the German

Clachan Publishing
3 Drumavoley Park, Ballycastle, BT54 6PE,
County Antrim.
ISBN: 978-1-909906-39-6

Email; info@clachanpublishing.com
Website: http://clachanpublishing-com.

This edition published 2016

Original edition London:
BRUCE AND WYLD. 1844.
34 Farrington Street, London:

Clachan
Publishing

Johann Georg Kohl

Johann Georg Kohl was born in Bremen in 1808, After studying he became a travel writer, visiting Russia in the 1830s and publishing his impressions soon after. The success of this work was followed by publications on Austria, England, Ireland, Wales and Scotland, the USA and Canada

His work on Ireland was published in 1844 and gives a glimpse of Irish life in the years after Catholic Emancipation in 1829 and immediately before the Great Irish Famine of 1845-1852 which resulted in the destruction of the last vestiges of the old Gaelic Ireland and the erosion of its language.

His journey took him through the four provinces including Dublin, Limerick, Waterford and Belfast. Part Four takes up the last stage of his journey From Drogheda, through County Down, Belfast and the Antrim Coast.

In the environs of Drogheda he reflects on the ancient origins of New Grange and the Irish watershed that was the Battle of the Boyne. He participates in a Gaelic evening of recitations and song, evoking the mythical characters of ancient Ireland. On entering County Down from the south, the neat orderliness of the Northeast is presented in stark contrast with the wretchedness he witnessed in the rest of rural Ireland. In Newry and Belfast he captures the sense of the rapid emergence of new world, brought about through enterprise and the newly mechanized linen industry. In contrast, his trip up the north coast road is a trip into the remnants of Gaelic Ireland, where he meets people who still speak Irish and tell tales of the fairies. His account of life on Rathlin Island and his speculations on the origin of the Giant's Causeway reveal the breadth of his informed interest in folklore and folkways as well as scientific investigation and the emerging scientific rationalism of his age.

Kohl's interest in the people, ballads and folklore of Ireland, gives us a glimpse of an aspect of life which had resisted colonial oppression only to be devastated by the great calamity of the Irish Famine which destroyed a vibrant peasant culture.

Contents

The Island of Rathlin   85

Cape Fair Head   94

The Giant's Causeway   103

The Bays and Headlands   118

Return and Conclusion   128

Index   133

Editor's Foreword

Clachan Publishing is a printing service dedicated to the preservation and promotion of print material related to Irish local and family histories. We produce books that are of local or family interest, such as memoires, articles, collections of old photographs, old letters, papers, newspaper cuttings, brochures, scrapbooks. We rely on materials given or lent to us by members of the public as well as commentaries and reports written by contemporaries of historic events.

The present publication is part of our series 'Local Histories'. It was first published in 1844 as part of a larger work called *Travels in Ireland*, also published by Clachan Publishing. Part Three contains the final chapters (from chapter 30 to 39) of this important work taking us through Drogheda, County Down, Belfast and the Antrim Coast and Giant's Causeway. Here we receive a picture of Ireland immediately prior to the Great Irish Famine (1845-1852), especially the emergence of Belfast and the liner industry.

Being in the public domain, we are happy to reproduce this book in print form and extend its readership in accordance with our mission to promote historic material of interest to local and family historians.

The text has been slightly edited in a manner that makes it more accessible to the modern reader. We have added explanatory footnotes that clarify obsolete and obscure references and turn of phrase. Also, some currency symbols, spelling, paragraphing and punctuation have been modernised. Furthermore, we have added an index to the original in order to help the reader navigate the text easily,

As this is a copy of an earlier publication, we cannot take responsibility for errors that may have occurred in the original. We wish to point out that the author's understandings reflect the views of his time, not present knowledge. This is relevant particularly to his understanding of the origin of round towers and the formation of the columns of the Giant's Causeway. We do however, take responsibility for any errors that may have resulted from the formatting and printing processes.

We make no claim to ownership of present or future copyright, but request that anyone who uses materials from this publication acknowledge both the original publication and this reproduction.

Seán O'Halloran, EDITOR, Clachan Publishing, January 2013.

From Dublin to Drogheda

'How Do You Spell Your Name, Sir?' — Cornishmen — Swords —
Balbriggan — The Beggars and my Fair Singing Companion — Linen Trade

In Germany, we sometimes say to a person whose name we do not know,
'May I take the liberty, sir, to ask you your name?' In England, one would
do better to say, 'How do you spell your name, sir?' otherwise one would
derive little information from the answer, which generally consists of some
corrupted, inarticulate sounds. 'How do you spell your name, sir?' asked I
of a man, who, having thrown his luggage into the well of the car, took his
seat on the bench beside me. I received a volley of letters in reply; but as I
was not yet sufficiently practised in English spelling, I was nothing the
wiser, for I neither knew how to write or to pronounce it. This much,
however, I know, by the final syllable *pen*, and the Christian name *John*, that
my friend must be from Cornwall; for of Cornishmen is sung the following
couplet: —

> By tre, pol, lan, and pen,
> You may know most Cornishmen.

These Cornishmen are usually called John, as the Welsh are Johnson: hence
the former say that the latter are their sons. Mr. [...]pen was a thorough
trader, and had no mind for any thing that was not in his *line*. When,
therefore, I told him I had come from Saxony, 'Ah, Saxony,' said he, 'that is
a very fine wool country!' When I expressed my regret that the weather was
bad, and that we would see but little of the interesting country, he replied,
'that all weathers were the same to him, if business were only doing; but the
worst of all was, that it was now so dull and slow.' 'But it is some
consolation to me,' said I, 'to think that we are entering on a better-
cultivated part of Ireland, and that the cultivation of the country and of the
people goes on increasing towards the north.' 'It is remarkable,' observed
he, 'that in like manner the linen and flax become finer and better as we
proceed northwards. That of Drogheda is not so fine as that of Newry; and
there are some places yet farther north where still finer articles are woven.'

All this conversation passed between us while we were making ourselves as
comfortable as we could on the car. At last we started off. The cloud of

---

poor invalids, beggars, useless helpers and helpers' helpers, and hawkers of newspapers and picture-books, all of whom were proclaiming in a loud voice the important novelties contained in their papers, to induce us to buy, cleared away, and our car, with its mountain of luggage, and its sixteen outside passengers, rolled off through the suburbs of Dublin. I remarked in passing, that here also a great number of houses were adorned with ivy, in the same manner as all ruins in Ireland. As Erin is the ivy-land, so is Dublin the ivy-city.

Under a heavy fall of hail, rain, and snow mixed together — a kind of weather which the English call *sleet*, and which is very common in Ireland — we drove past the ruins of the cathedral of Swords. There stood beside them a large and almost perfect Round Tower, and many lordly old trees. The name Swords, although English, reminded me of the old Irish battles fought by Erin's king, Brian Boru.

Farther on we passed another ruin, the old castle of Balruddery; but at the next town, Balbriggan, quite a spectacle presented itself to me — a large manufactory! Balbriggan was the first place in Ireland in which I found a great cotton-mill. Balbriggan stockings are celebrated, even in England. From this place the north-eastern manufacturing district of Ireland may be said to begin. The ruins cease to be the principal objects of interest; and such grand groups of ruins as those of Kilkenny, Glendalough, and Cashel, are no longer to be met with in the north.

We took a little siesta at Balbriggan, and changed our horses. As we again seated ourselves on the car, we were surrounded by the usual swarm of poor people, begging us for Heaven's sake to give them a halfpenny. 'There's time enough yet, gentlemen! the car's just going off!' exclaimed they, as the driver raised his whip. 'There's time enough yet, your honours! Sure your honours won't go away without leaving us and our poor families a trifle! I'm not asking for myself, your honours, but for my poor dying children! Oh! oh! the car is going off, and your honours won't give us any thing!' In the meantime it had become dark. It is by no means pleasant to be on an Irish car when night comes on, without the light of either stars or moon, as was now our case; for one cannot venture to sleep through fear of tumbling off. A stout lady, who sat at the other side of me, therefore after a while began to sing aloud. She said she did so to keep herself awake and lively. Accompanied by her song and our universal dumbness, both of which, as well as the rough sleet, continued all the way to Drogheda, we entered the last-named town.

In this entire district, and particularly in Drogheda, the linen manufacture is the staple trade of the inhabitants. In consequence, however, of the erection of extensive flax spinning-mills at Leeds, this branch of Irish commerce has of late greatly decreased, and the linen manufacture is now much depressed. In England, it is one of the most recent branches of its manufacturing activity; whilst in Ireland it is one of the oldest. The linen manufacture of Ireland has occupied the attention of the English and Irish legislatures for two hundred years; but in England it has only obtained importance since the beginning of the present century, in consequence of the introduction of vast spinning-machines. These machines have also been lately introduced into Ireland, and the flax-spinning is now conducted on quite a new system. Many towns have been losers, and others gainers, by this change. It is remarkable that the exportation of Irish linen to England and foreign countries since the beginning of the present century, has regularly fluctuated between thirty-five and fifty-five millions of yards yearly. The general lamentations of the linen manufacturers and flax-spinners, that their trade has been destroyed, may therefore probably be caused by the increase of population, and of hands seeking employment. The population of Ireland has almost doubled itself since 1800; and to prevent these lamentations, the production and exportation of linen should also have been doubled in the same period.

Drogheda and its Environs

Drogheda is an old Irish place, but is almost entirely in the style of English
towns. It is the only town in the north of Ireland the population of which is
on the decrease. In 1821 it had 18,118, and in 1831, only 17,365 inhabitants.
It is situated on the Boyne, which has become famous, less for its slightly
dark-coloured bog-water, — one of its chief tributaries is called the
Blackwater, a name borne and deserved by many rivers of Ireland — than
for the blood that was once poured into it. The famous — for the English,
the glorious, by the Irish, the deplored — Battle of the Boyne, in which
William III. conquered James II., and drove him from the country, was
fought here. This battle was to the Irish what the battle of the White
Mountain was to the Bohemians, and the battle of Culloden to the Scots.
The battle-field lies up the river, a few miles from Drogheda; and as the
valley is distinguished as well by its natural charms, as, in particular, by its
Druidical remains, and, above all, by the celebrated sepulchral monument
of New Grange, I made a little journey up along the river on the following
day, in company with a well-informed and kind patriot of Drogheda.

In a narrow part of the valley, where the struggle that decided the battle
took place, there has been erected an obelisk, on a little block of stone, or
rock, close by the river. My friend, who had grown up in the
neighbourhood, informed me, that, at the present moment, all the details of
the battle live in the memories of the people who dwell around, and are
handed down from generation to generation; and not these particulars

4

alone, but all the high relationships and entire genealogies of the distinguished personages who were engaged in it. The Irish traditions still possess the peculiar precise character of the traditions of nations who have no books, and whose memory is therefore the stronger. In them every thing is described with the greatest accuracy, — the localities, the physiognomies, the speeches, — just as if the people had seen every thing themselves. Among those who fell at the battle of the Boyne were several Germans, who accompanied William from Holland, one of whom, the Duke Schomberg, commanded a part of William's troops. The people here say that the German troops had offered violence to an Irish country girl, for which her lover swore he would take revenge: but being unable to discover the actual miscreants, he selected their general, and slew him.

James II. behaved with no great bravery in this memorable battle, which was fought on the 1st of July, 1690. Seized by a panic, even while the battle was yet undecided, he sought safety in flight, and rode through the entire length of the island, at a pace that has never been equalled. In a few hours he had left behind him the entire way from the battle-field to Dublin Castle; and on the next evening he rode to Waterford, a distance of more than one hundred English miles. The Irish therefore justly call him *Shamus a' cacach*, that is, cowardly, or dirty James. On his part, James threw all the blame on the Irish; for when, in his flight, he reached the Castle of Dublin, and Lady Tyrconnell, a woman of ready wit, came out to meet him, he said to her, 'Your countrymen, the Irish, madam, can run very quick;' her reply was, 'Your majesty excels them in this, as in every thing else, for you have won the race.' At Waterford, James embarked for France. As he was in the act of ascending the side of the ship, the wind blew off his hat; and as it was evening, and the hat could not be recovered immediately, his attendant, General O'Farrell, an Irishman, put his own hat on him, that he might not take cold. James was pleased, and remarked, as he ascended the vessel, that if, through the fault of the Irish, he had lost a crown, he had gained a hat from them in its place. James's accusations of the swift-footedness of the Irish are now forgotten; but the Irish still blame him, and have not ceased to call him a' cacach. By this battle William III. confirmed, for the last time, Henry II.'s conquest, the subjection of Ireland, — a subjection which before this had to be confirmed once or twice every century by an English army. In the centre of Ireland two new counties were formed, and were called, in honour of William and his consort, the King's County and the Queen's County.

The entire valley of the Boyne, from Drogheda as far as *Navan*, contains traces of Druidical monuments. Thus, on our way, we inspected the remains of a cromlech or Druidical circular temple, which is situated on a height. It now consists of only four large stones, disposed in the form of a segment of a circle. As a part of the height had been dug away for agricultural purposes, two other stories had sunk down. Farther up the valley are several large tumuli, one of which is the celebrated hill of New Grange. This hill, which is composed of an enormous mass of flint-stones, is about 50 or 60 feet high, and 200 paces in circumference. The multitude of stones of which it is formed is therefore immensely great, especially as most of them, at least those on the summit, are not much larger than common paving-stones. Round about the hill, at the edge of its base, is a circle of large blocks of stone, the heads of which are all stuck into the ground. Some of these stones have already fallen; others have completely disappeared. As the hill is surrounded by arable land, the peasants may have removed many of the stones to make way for the plough, so that the circle is no longer complete. The outside of the hill is now entirely overgrown with grass, bushes, and trees, the stones having, in the course of years, become covered with dust, mould, and clay, on which vegetation then sprang up. Here and there, however, particularly upon the summit, this green covering of grass has been removed, probably to satisfy the curiosity of man; and there the stones may be plainly seen, as well as every where else, by any one who takes the trouble to dig away the soil.

In size and outward shape, this tumulus closely resembles those which have been raised at Cracow, in honour of Kosciuzko, Wanda, and Krak. It also reminds one of the tumulus of Elpenor, and of that of Achilles, on the Sigaean promontory, as described by travellers, and by Homer in the twelfth book of his Odyssey. The mound of Patroclus, and that of Halyattes in Asia Minor, according to Camden's testimony, must be very like it. The larger of the Tartaric tumuli in the Crimea, which were probably erected in honour of Scythian or Bosphoran kings, exactly resemble it in figure, with this difference, that, in that stoneless country, they are composed, not of stones, but of earth. In the south of Russia, on the top of these mounds a figure, rudely chiselled out of stone, is sometimes placed, or even a common stone. On the tumulus of Achilles, too, traces of a pillar are said to be still visible; and in Ireland it is affirmed that, in like manner, great blocks of stone stood on them, as final or top stones. On the summit of these mounds there is generally found a little hollow, in which the stone stood, and out of which it may have been washed away by the rain. The English call these mounds barrows when built of earth, and cairns when built of stones.

It is not, however, in its exterior appearance, but in its internal structure, that the hill of New Grange is most interesting. An opening has been discovered at the base of the hill, through which the hollow interior may be reached, and this was the principal object of our journey. For this purpose we had provided ourselves with lights, the entrance being extremely narrow and rather long. Before the entrance there is a little space protected from the wind, a kind of cave in the earth heaped up at the foot of the mound, and which was probably formed by the explorers and excavators of the entrance. Here we took off our clothes, lighted our candles, and commenced our operations. The passage, which is about fifty feet long, is somewhat obstructed with stones, so that one can only work his way in by lying on his back, while he feels his way with his feet, and pushes himself forward with his hands. As the ground is covered with sharp-cornered flint-stones, this slide-path is not the most agreeable in the world. The sidewalls of the passage are formed of large, tolerably flat stones, set up perpendicularly, with equally large stones laid across them on the top. We soon reached the convenient interior of the tumulus, where one can not only stand upright, but can also walk about freely, as it is neither more nor less than a little chapel, to which three side-chapels are appended. Having brought with us a whole bundle of candles, we hung one of them in the centre of the large chapel, another in each of the three small ones, and the remainder we attached round about to the rocks, wherever we could; and now, in this illumination, my eyes beheld the most remarkable and most interesting specimen of primitive Cyclopean architecture I ever saw. Rude and simple as every thing was, it would yet be difficult for me to convey to my readers a correct idea of the appearance and structure of these chapels.

It is manifest that they were not hollowed out of the mound of stones subsequent to its erection, for this its structure would not permit; but they existed before the hill itself, and the great pyramid of flint-stones, was raised over the roof of the chapels. As children build houses of cards, so were these chapels built of blocks of stones. A few large flat stones were placed beside one another, on their edges, to form the back and side walls, and over them a few more were placed to make a ceiling. In this way were the three little side-chapels constructed. They of course remained open on the side where they were to communicate with the centre larger chapel. One of these chapels faces the east, one the west, and one the north; on the south is the entrance to the passage out. This opening is a door, with gigantic stone door-posts and stone architraves. The principal difficulty the old Cyclopean architects had to surmount must have been in the construction of the vaulted roof of the high middle chapel; and this difficulty has been solved by supposing that, upon the four firm bases or points of support afforded by the roofs of the little chapels and the mighty architraves of the door-way of the centre one, they laid other large flat pieces of rock, which projected inwards a little. On these again they placed similar stones, which projected inwards a little more than those beneath them, and thus gradually narrowed the space more and more. This operation was repeated three or four times, so that at last only a small hole remained open in the top of the centre chapel, which was then closed by one gigantic stone, and in this way the whole was completed. When the chapel was afterwards covered outside with a mass of flint-stones, their weight gave increased firmness to the over-lapping stones that formed the roof, and in this way the entire building must remain there, firm and indestructible, through eternity. The immense mass of stones which now lies, like a great hill, upon this chapel and its side-chapels, and upon the roof of the entrance-passage, was probably formed gradually, and in the course of time. It was and is the custom, not only in Arabia, some countries of Africa, and many others of the world, but also in Ireland and in Scotland, to heap up stones on holy places, and particularly over graves. In Arabia, in northern Africa, in some of the Baltic Provinces, as in Esthonia, and also in some parts of Scotland, usage requires every one who passes by to throw a stone upon the holy place, while he probably at the same time makes some pious wish, or repeats a short prayer. In this way great heaps of stones have been raised, in various places, in all these countries. It is probable that, immediately on the consecration of the holy place, a great portion of the stones were thrown upon it by the assembled multitude; and afterwards, in the course of centuries the original heap became a hill, a result of the pious labours of the believing.

I have said that in this way the entire Cyclopean work will endure for eternity; for, excepting the wasting away of the stones by the action of the air and weather, which, from the hardness of their nature, cannot happen in any conceivable period of time, no cause can be imagined capable of destroying these monuments. The thousands of years which have passed over these stones have not left on them a single trace of injury. A gnawing moss-plant has not even once fixed itself inside. An earthquake, opening the mouth of the earth, and swallowing up the entire monument, is the only conceivable natural event that could destroy this chapel. But Ireland has not yet suffered this calamity, and probably never will. In all probability, it has as little to fear from man as from nature; for none of the motives which have led to the destruction of ancient buildings can exist with regard to New Grange. Many of our architectural remains have disappeared beneath the destroying hand of man, because they became obnoxious to succeeding generations. Thus were destroyed the Bastille at Paris, and many an old German castle and town. Many were demolished because their materials could be applied by succeeding generations to other purposes. Others were destroyed to satisfy avarice and curiosity, because their destroyers hoped to find either treasures or other matters concealed in them. Thus several pyramids in Egypt, several royal sepulchers in the Crimea, and in other places, have been rummaged and destroyed. Then, again, passion for art and science has all but ruined other monuments, as witness many beautiful temples in Greece. Of all these motives, however, not one can arm the inhabitants of Erin against such monuments as New Grange. Great blocks of stone, such as these, can be of no use to the present or future generations; unless the human race again returns to its old barbarism, and our architectural arts descend to the level of this Cyclopean architecture. And, even then, blocks of stone, more easily obtainable, would be found in the neighbourhood.

These chapels can no longer in any way be offensive; for the differences of opinion, and the party contentions, of which they were perhaps once the object, in the time of the Druids, just as many heathen and not-heathen temples afterwards became, and still are, have all long since passed away, and their revival is altogether inconceivable. Mere wantonness would have far too much to do in the destruction of these vast masses of stone, so that we need not entertain any fears from that cause. The art-enthusiasts, who have plundered the temples of Greece and of other countries, can scarcely

---

find any thing here worth robbing; for these structures are only remarkable in their present entirety, and would lose their interest as soon as the individual pieces were taken asunder. Perhaps an exception must be made to this in a few respects, as I will immediately show. Curiosity and avarice can derive little or nothing from the destruction of this edifice; for here there is nothing hidden from the sight, and every one can immediately convince himself that it contains nothing more than the rude masses of stone before his eyes. From all this it follows, that New Grange, like other similar monuments of a remote antiquity, will most probably last longer than the tower of Babylon, the obelisks of Egypt, the temples of Greece, the castles of the middle ages, and all the buildings of our own day. This reflection at once forces itself on the spectator; and, while it fills him with respect for these witnesses of a long-departed age, convinces him that they will continue to speak into as far distant a future.

We then examined the details of the three little chapels, and found them no less interesting than the structure of the whole. In each of them we saw a large stone basin, and, in one of them, two such basins, one within the other. These basins, which bear some resemblance to the baptismal fonts of our Christian churches, are the most remarkable specimens of Druidical or Cyclopean stone-cutting I ever beheld. They are great caldron-round stones, about twenty or twenty-four feet in circumference, hollowed out into a shallow cavity, like the saucer of a tea-cup. The manner in which they were hollowed out, and the entire workmanship of them, is so rude, and the circular form of the basin is so irregular, that, although it is quite evident they have been thus fashioned, not by nature but by art, it is yet impossible to conceive in what way this form has been given then. Chisel, circle, and measuring-rod seem not to have been used in their formation. It looks just as if the hollows were produced by rubbing one great stone upon another for a long time. These basins rest upon another immense stone, which serves them as a pedestal; and in the eastern chapel there is, as I have said, two such basins, a smaller within a larger. Perhaps in the other two chapels there were also similar little basins, which may have been removed for some museum of antiquities; for I remember having seen a Druidical basin of this kind in an English museum. The northern chapel, which is exactly opposite the entrance-passage, is constructed of the largest stones. One of the basins was half-full of water which had trickled from the roof of the cavern. My companion told me that he always saw this water here, whenever he visited the chapel.

With the exception of these basins, few traces of art are to be seen, and these consist of some marks here and there on the stones. On one, for example, several parallel zigzag lines have been cut. On the surface of another are some spiral lines, winding round in six or seven circles, within one another, like a helix. Then there are some little round figures with radii, which resemble stars, and, finally, a figure which seems to be meant for an imitation of flowers or fruits. Those star-like figures were perhaps meant for stars, which the old star-worshipping Druids used to engrave upon the tombs of their heroes. All these things are very awkwardly, rudely, and by no means deeply cut. The spiral lines are the most numerous, and reminded me of the many spirals of metal wire which have been found in very old tombs, and which are supposed to have been intended for ornaments. An inscription, too, is shown in one of the chapels, on the foot of one of its side-stones. It consists of various undecipherable characters, which, as Irish antiquarians assert, belong neither to the Feadha, the common old Irish alphabet, nor to the Ogham, the secret writing of the ancient Irish; but is, in all probability, an apocryphal addition of modern date. The most remarkable evidence of human labour, however, is on a stone which forms the inner door-post of the chapel. The projecting edge of this stone is marked, from top to bottom, with slight grooves or furrows. It appears precisely as if several ropes had been for a long time drawn backwards and forwards across it, and worn in it one furrow over another. When we consider the size of the stone, this marking must have cost no slight trouble, and it is quite impossible to conjecture its object. Were these furrows intended for numerical records? The entire structure and its details, is, in fact, one of the most interesting sights one can behold. It is to be regretted that this temple is so concealed, and that, by reason of its inconvenient entrance, it is almost inaccessible to half the human race — the fair sex. Were the managers of the opera of *Norma* acquainted with this subterranean Druid-temple, they would certainly have represented it on the stage, and it could scarcely fail to make a great impression on the spectators.

As we were going out again, and I once more threw the light on some stones, I observed, on those which formed the inner-door of the entrance, a countless multitude of little gnats. These animals are now the only, and perhaps the most ancient, inhabitants of this colossal work. Year after year they retire here in the autumn to pass the winter, and fly out again in the spring.

When at last we regained the open air, we met two Irish peasants, and asked them by whom they believed these caverns were formed. They replied 'the Danes,' which is the usual answer given by the Irish to questions respecting the origin of any ancient structure in their country. It is the Danes who have piled up their moats, the Danes to whom the oldest of their ruined castles are attributed, the Danes have erected the ancient barrows and cairns. Even the Round Towers, the ignorant common people sometimes ascribe to the Danes; and, in fact, to the annoyance of the inquisitive tourist and the friend of antiquity, there are even many among the well-educated, who, without further reflection, repeat this opinion of the people. The Danes were in Ireland in the ninth, tenth, and eleventh centuries; while many of the monuments attributed to them manifestly derive their origin from a far earlier period. Besides, they properly occupied only the eastern part of the island; while the monuments ascribed to them are, on the contrary, found in all parts of it, and are so extremely numerous, and of such variety, that one cannot avoid concluding that the people are in error. But, on the other hand, the Irish are not deficient in boldness of imagination, as they often date their traditions from a far more remote period than that of the Danes. Nay, they are even inclined, wherever possible, to ascend centuries back, before their time; and therefore it would seem that they are entitled to some belief in relation to their Danish monuments, when they content themselves with claiming for them a date comparatively modern.

All these various considerations combined have led me to an hypothesis which I have met with in no Irish writer, namely, that the Irish people may have confounded the Danes with the much more ancient nation, of nearly the same name, the Danaans, who are said to have lived in Ireland long before the birth of Christ. These Danaans, or Tuatha-de-Danaans, were, according to Irish tradition, the third race who colonised Ireland. Of these Danaans, Moore, who repeats the popular tradition, says: — 'They were a people famed for necromancy, who, after sojourning for some time in Greece, where they had learned this mysterious art, proceeded from thence to Denmark and Norway, and became possessors, while in those countries, of certain marvelous treasures, among which were the Stone of Destiny, the

12

Sorcerer's Spear, and the Magic Caldron. Armed with these wonderful gifts, the tribe of the Danaans next found their way to Scotland; and, after a rest there of some years, set sail, under the auspices of their chieftain, Nuad of the Silver Hand[1], for Ireland. Here, landing secretly, under cover of a mist which their enchantments had raised, these sorcerers penetrated into the country, and conquered the inhabitants in the battle of Moytura, which is also called the 'Battle of the Field of the Tower."

As so much art, and even magic, is attributed to the Danaans, they may have easily covered Ireland with many monuments of their skill; and as their name has nearly the same sound as that of the Danes, the generations which dwelt in Ireland after the Danes may have given the latter credit for much that properly belonged to that more ancient people. Moreover, most of the remains of the Danes, or Danaans, are, even at the present moment, objects of superstition, and the scenes of goblins and enchantment! So much is certain, that Cyclopean structures, like this of New Grange, must date their origin from the most remote antiquity. It is likewise highly probable, and now the generally-received opinion among the learned, that these barrows and cairns served for some religious purpose. Some believe that they were the sepulchral monuments of celebrated heroes or kings. Others imagine that they were temples. Perhaps they may have served both purposes at the same time. In Africa, there are tribes who have no other temples, or places for prayer, than the graves of their Marabouts. In these subterraneous chapels, perhaps, not only were sacrifices offered up to the memory and the manes[2] of the revered departed, a king or a high-priest, but also the well-being of all was implored in prayer, while on the summit of the hill a fire was kindled in honour of the Sun-god, or god of light. In Cornwall there is a cairn called Karn Leskyg, or 'Karn of Burnings'. Perhaps the summit was sacred to the celestial Sun-god, or god of light, and

---

[1] 'So called,' says Moore, 'from an artificial silver hand, which he wore to supply the loss sustained from a wound he received in the battle of Moytura. We are told seriously by O'Flaherty, that Cred, a goldsmith, formed the hand, and Miach, the son of Dian Kect, well instructed in the practical parts of chirurgery, set the arm!' I add this merely to give my readers some idea of the extraordinary accuracy of detail with which the Irish write their imaginative history. [original footnote].

[2] spirits of ancestors, [Clachan ed.].

the hollow subterranean chapels, on the contrary, to the infernal powers. The stone basins may then have served for altars, or sacrificial vessels.

There are, as I have said, many other tumuli along the banks of the Boyne, yet they are all, with one exception, far lower and smaller than that of New Grange. The people say that ancient chieftains are buried beneath these little hills. The exception is that called Dowth, or the Moat of Dowth, which exactly resembles New Grange; but it seems to me to be a little larger and higher, and outside it is not covered with bushes, but quite bare. At one spot, where the turf has been removed, one can plainly see that, like New Grange, it is composed of an immense mass of flint stones. On one side of the hill there is also an entrance, a couple of large stones, laid on one another, forming just such a door as that of New Grange. It is extremely probable that this entrance leads to a similar hollow passage, and again to a chapel, perhaps larger, perhaps somewhat varied, and at all events interesting for the sake of comparison. But, oh! disgrace to all those inhabitants of the surrounding country, with their ten thousands a year! — the entrance has not been opened any farther, and nothing is yet known of the interior. I remember well how I abused the barbarism of the country, when I beheld, in southern Russia and among the Tartars, the many yet untouched and unopened tumuli. But should I go there again I will beg pardon of the people for this injustice, since, in a state like Great Britain, such extremely interesting and remarkable monuments stand unexamined, yes, unvalued, silent, and shut up, like the Pyramids in the desert. Would not one imagine that here, in this English country, every thing worth examining would be explored and rummaged, over and over again, by antiquarians, and lovers of science and art? But I must add, that the cairn or temple of Dowth is not the only instance of this kind.

From the summit of this hill we enjoyed one of the most beautiful prospects of the valley of the Boyne, down upon all the tumuli lying around, upon the river winding between them, and then away towards the west upon the town of Slane, where, in former times, a famous college existed, and which still lies there, as Cromwell left it — in ruins. To these old Catholic colleges, now lying in rubbish, the Irish patriots point with sadness. They once had many of them; but since the times of Cromwell and of William III. they have none. Their young people, intended for the priesthood, were all forced to complete their clerical education in foreign lands, in Spain, Italy, or France. Not till a recent period did the Roman

Catholics obtain a college of their own for the education of their clergy — the College of Maynooth in the vicinity of Dublin, which now represents the university of Roman Catholic Ireland.

Not far from the Moat of Dowth, upon the estate of the Netterville family, are the ruins of an old church. They are, as usual, ornamented with ivy; and within the roofless circuit of its walls are, as is also usual, the monuments of those who, as the Irish say, 'were brought home to their own people.' Among others was the white marble monument of a Netterville, which stood so extremely pleasing and picturesque between the gray church-walls and the green ivy, that I cannot understand why the English travel to Père la Chaise at Paris, and to Frankfort, to see the prosaic monuments there, while, by making a tour of the old churchyards of Ireland, they might enjoy the greatest abundance of picturesque, beautiful, and in every respect interesting sights. We have many complete collections of all distinguished English mansions: why have not a few English painters and writers joined, and given to the world an illustrated work under the title of 'The Old Churchyards of Ireland?' The painter indeed must be a Ruysdael, whose unequalled *Churchyard*, in the Royal Gallery at Dresden, comes near in effect and poetry to an Irish churchyard; while the writer must be a Moore or a Byron, for the aesthetic as well as the historical department should be illumined with liveliness and imagination. These churchyards, in which, amid ruins and beneath venerable trees, often in the midst of the greatest wildness and desolation, the noble and the poor are buried, are unquestionably the most significant symbols of the condition and mode of thinking of the Irish people. The Irish are much attached to every thing that is old, and imagine that they can find their last long rest only among the dust of 'their own people,' and in that place with which so many old traditions and legends are associated, although these witnesses of the days of their ancient glory now lie in ruin and decay. Full of love for their old churches, for their old traditions, for their old recollections, generations after generations lay themselves down here amid these shattered walls, and seem to hope that Ireland too, as well as themselves, will one day arise from her ruins to a new and glorious life.

I visited this church, however, not on account of the old monuments, but for something else, — namely, *Shilagh na Gigh*[1], that is, in English, '*Cicely of the Branch,*' whose name relates to an extremely remarkable old Irish custom, which again reminded me of the East — this time the old East of Herodotus. The Irish are no less superstitious than the Romans of old, and, like them, 'ill luck and good luck' is the principal object of their thoughts and cares. A hundred thousand things and events are signs of 'ill luck:' meetings, looks, words, sounds, natural phenomena, feelings of various kinds, become signs of ill luck under certain circumstances. The look of a sorceress is especially dreaded. 'She overlooked my child, and it now fades in his bloom,' is the expression used on such occasions.

As in nature every poison has its antidote, so likewise, in the world of Irish superstition, there are as many things that bring *good luck* as there are that bring *bad luck*. For good luck they spit upon the penny they receive, lest it may be enchanted and infected with ill luck. For good luck they dip their children in holy wells, or have recourse to various charms, when the ill luck of a look or of a mere word is upon them. Even adults, even men, have sometimes a dark and melancholy feeling that a spell of ill luck has been thrown around them by some person or other; and, among the various remedies they adopt to counteract it 'for good luck,' is this: — '*Persuadent nempe mulierem, ut exhibeat iis quod mulieres secretissimum habent*[2].'

There once were — and whatever was once in Ireland, one may be almost certain that it is still there — women, who made a profession of this, and who, whenever a young or old man was tormented by the idea of *ill luck*, permitted him to try this means for *good luck*. These women were, and are still, called Shilagh na Gigh: the origin of this name I have not been able to learn. It may be, however, that the belief gained ground that the mere image would be sufficient; and the priests, so thought an Irishman whom I questioned on this subject, did all in their power to increase this belief, in order to diminish the use of the original remedy itself. Female images were therefore made to answer the purpose of living women, and were also called Shilagh na Gigh. They were built into the side-walls of the chapels,

---

[1] A carving of a woman with exposed genitalia, usually found on religious buildings, [Clachan ed.].

[2] They persuaded the woman to show that these women have a secret. [Lat] , [Clachan ed.].

probably in order that thus they might be the more potent. My companion, who was intimately acquainted with Irish customs and antiquities, assured me that he knew of ten or eleven old chapels with these figures, and that one of them was still to be seen in the southern wall of the above-mentioned chapel of the Nettervilles. To convince myself of this, I went there, and after some search I found a little female figure in the place described. It was chiselled out of one of the stones of the wall, in low relief, "nuda erat, nec non exhibuit, quod juvenes 'for good luck's sake' spectare optarent."[1] My companion remarked, 'they call it also a female exhibition.' I thought of the women whom Herodotus says frequented the temple at Babylon, partly perhaps also 'for good luck.'

Here is another proof that this western island is full of peculiarities to be met with in no other country of Europe. Look whatever way one will, he will find some in Ireland. Thus, on our return to Drogheda, we met a funeral, and it struck me that the bier was very rudely constructed. On inquiry, the people told me that little art was here employed on the bier, because it was never used more than once, but immediately after the burial it was broken to pieces, and thrown into the grave. I afterwards found that this custom was pretty general in the north of Ireland. They destroy it in the churchyard, either by hewing it with a hatchet, or placing it between the forked limbs of a tree, and thus breaking it to pieces.

I had scarcely entered Drogheda at one side, before I had again to quit it on the other, in consequence of the resolution of some enthusiastic friends of antiquity, with whom I had the good luck to become acquainted in that place, and who would not suffer me to depart until I enjoyed a sight of their celebrated Monasterboice. These (in Ireland) famous monastic ruins lie a few miles to the north of Drogheda, and I set out for them the next day. They consisted of the remains of some churches, and a Round Tower, and are some distance from the high road, so that we had to reach the lonely and deserted pile by narrow by-ways. Monasterboice, or, as it is called in the Irish language, 'Mainistir-Buite', i.e. the Monastery of Buite or Boetius, owes its origin to a celebrated abbot or bishop of that name, who lived towards the close of the fifth century, and was a disciple of St. Patrick.

---

[1] she did not exhibit, that which the young men 'for good luck's sake' have desired his look at. [Lat] , [Clachan ed.].

Many abbots and professors of this monastery distinguished themselves, and are all famous in Irish annals. The most celebrated of them was Flann, who died in the year 1056. He was the last great original authority of the old Irish language, in history, poetry, and eloquence, says his biographer *Adamnán*; and of him it is also said —

> Flann, of the great church of sweet Buite,
> The last professor the country of the three Finns was Flann.

There is said to be still extant a multitude of historical poems written by him. But the work for which he is most celebrated in Ireland, is his *Synchronisms* of the Irish kings, and of the Oriental and Roman emperors, and the head monarchs of all Ireland, as well as its Christian provincial rulers, and, finally, the kings of Scotland of Irish descent.

Monasterboice, in remote times so long the seat of piety, art, science, and learning, lost its importance and fell into ruins after the English took possession of the kingdom of Meath, to which it belonged.

Not far from the ruins, on a bleak height, lay a few huts of Irish labourers; and then the road led down into the plain, in which nothing was to be seen but these ruins in the centre. They lie together, lonely and melancholy, in a picturesque group; and while all around was bare, they were overshadowed by some old trees, which found support and protection between their walls. At the side of the high Round Tower, around whose lofty broken summit ravens and rooks were fluttering, and between the low ivy-mantled church-walls, a couple of lofty stone crosses showed themselves, erect and uninjured, while the intermediate spaces, as usual, were filled with old and falling, and new and upright, gravestones. The dusky hue of the turfy soil around, the bright-yellow foliage of the trees amid the ruins, and the green sward at the base of the buildings, all these various colours gave an extremely picturesque appearance to the interesting group of little crosses, churches, tower, and gravestones. Then there was no one to be seen, except myself and the guide whom I had chosen at the huts; and the entire sky, as is usual in Ireland, was full of cloud-mountains of the vastest and most grotesque shapes.

I here again felt the truth of an Irish writer (Petrie)[1], who, describing the Irish landscape, says, — 'The colours with which nature has painted the surface of Erin, are quite peculiar to our island. There is not a shade of green which does not adorn her soil, from the brightest yellow-green to the darkest brown-green. In no other land are these colours of equal strength and depth. Even our bogs, with all their variations of colours, with their purple, their red, brown, black, by their violent contrasts add still more beauty to it, and complete the national individuality of our landscape. Nay, even our clouds, too, have in a high degree a quite peculiar character, which is the result of the moisture of our climate. They have a vastness in their forms and shapes, a strength of light and shade, seldom seen in other lands. Irish clouds are one moment sunny and glittering, and in the next moment they are rolling their dark shadows over the landscape, and shrouding it in melancholy gloom.' These words of another clearly express what every traveller in Ireland will see, especially what he says respecting the clouds. Ireland is the richest cloud-land in Europe, and every painter should come here to study clouds. This is also partly true of the whole islands of Great Britain, and explains why, in the works of all English landscape painters, such great attention, such detailed execution, and so much trouble is bestowed on the sky; and also why Howard, the first who attempted a classification of clouds, was an Englishman.

What I have remarked respecting the clouds, might be also said symbolically of the political and moral heaven of Erin. As clouds upon clouds rise from the Atlantic Ocean, and envelope her in an ever-varying and ever differently tattered mantle of gloom, with beams of light flowing down through the rents, so clouds upon clouds continually emerge from the sea of events, and shroud in constantly-changing forms the oppressed and straitened spirit of her people, who dream on in sad despair, being but occasionally permitted, in the warm sunshine of prosperity and joy, to resign themselves to a passing ecstasy. One cannot help believing that he perceives the character of a people, and the national history of their country, depicted in the natural scenery and climate of their land. These changing clouds of an Irish sky continually remind us of Moore's poems: —

---

[1] George Petrie (1 January 1790 – 1866), referred to as the father of Irish archeology, was also a painter, musician and collector of Irish songs,

Erin! the tear and the smile in thine eyes,
Blend like the rainbow that hangs in thy skies!
of his shades of sorrow:
Has sorrow thy young days shaded.
of his sun-gleams of joy:
As a beam o'er the face of the waters may glow!
of his weeping stars:
At the mid-hour of night, when the stars are weeping.
of his lingering and vanishing light:
'Tis gone, and for ever, the light we saw breaking.
of his sunbeams amid rain:
Though dark are our sorrows, to-day we'll forget them,
And smile through our tears, like a sunbeam in showers.

We at length arrived at the ruins themselves; and at the same time there also arrived one of those stormy hail-showers, rolling over the landscape. The hail rattled down between the old shattered walls, and we had to creep for shelter into the Round Tower, the door of which was here fortunately near enough to the ground to allow us to slip in with ease. This tower is of the usual height of 110 feet, but may have been somewhat higher, as its summit is now broken. It has also the usual circumference of 50 feet. Though I was always glad to be able to visit one of these singular buildings, I found nothing in this tower of Monasterboice to distinguish it from others of the same kind. The ruined churches likewise have nothing to distinguish them, beyond the picturesque charms common to all Irish ruins. Here, however, are the three remarkable crosses I have already mentioned, erected in honour of the three celebrated Irish saints, St. Patrick, Boetius, and Columb Kill.

These crosses belong to the most remarkable of the old Christian antiquities of Ireland, being decorated with great art, and better preserved than others of a similar description. They are composed of several large blocks of stone, laid one over another, are from twenty to twenty-four feet high, and are ornamented from top to bottom with graceful sculptures. Their form is quite peculiar, and in no Christian country have I seen any thing like them. On a pillar, about fourteen feet high, which stands on a broad pedestal, is fixed a cross, with four arms of equal length, each of which becomes somewhat wider towards the centre, in the same manner as the cross of the Knights of Malta; the arms of the cross are bound by a large stone ring or circle, the segments of which pass from arm to arm. It looks as if a stone cross and a stone ring were united into one figure. The pillars, crosses, rings, all are covered with sculptures, which afford plenty of subjects for thought to the Irish antiquary. Their whole appearance proves that a very peculiar style of Christian art existed in ancient Ireland; and, by the manner of their lines and drawings, reminded me of the paintings and embellishments of the old Irish manuscripts which I had seen at the college library in Dublin. The pillars and the arms of the cross are, of course, four-sided; each side is bordered with twisted lines or spirals; and the entire is divided into little squares, in each of which is a scene from the *Old* or *New Testament* history; for instance, Adam and Eve, Cain and Abel, Paradise, Hell, the Passion, &c. In Paradise, I remarked a couple of harpers. The Irishman could not conceive a Paradise, in which he could not find his beloved national instrument.

The spiral borders and the ornaments, which serve here and there to fill up, are quite peculiar. Thus, on one cross I saw intertwined snakes, winding round a human head; on another, a woman with a long dog hanging to each ear, — perhaps a scene of torture from the Irish hell. Two dogs, of slender forms, twisted into a very peculiar figure, almost like snakes, occurred very often. I could not learn the meaning of these dogs, which appear so frequently on the old Christian monuments of Ireland. At Dublin, I saw a crosier, which was covered all over with these slender little dogs, wrought on the back of its crook. They probably refer to the legend of some Irish saint.

A very peculiar drawing, which I had already noticed on several Irish antiquities, again presented itself to me on Columba's cross, and on that of St. Patrick. It was a perfectly regular circle, in which many twisted, wavy, and spiral lines were intertwined. On one of these circles was a hand, neatly chiselled, in bas-relief, upon the stone.

I began to consider what the monks could have meant by these signs, unquestionably symbolical; and when I could not find any thing better, I conceived that by the circle they perhaps intended to signify the globe of the world; by the twisted and knotted, snaky and spiral lines, the various and stormy eddies and whirlpools of human life and passions, which flow through that globe; while the hand, lying upon it, represented the hand of the Creator and Father of all things, who rules all these confused lines, and will one day reduce them all into harmonious order. When I had finished this solution, I asked my attendant Paddy his opinion respecting the hand, and the circle beneath it? Taking off his hat, he replied: 'I'll tell your honour. Look! there was a woman who baked a cake one Sunday, and broke the commandment: but when she caught hold of the cake to take it up, it remained hanging to her hand, and she could never get it off again; and the holy St. Patrick therefore had it carved on the stone here, to remind and to warn us for ever to keep holy the holydays and Sundays, as we are commanded. That's it, your honour!' added Paddy, and he put on his hat again.

On the foot of one cross various monsters are carved, probably symbolic of heathenism and the foes of Christianity, in the midst of which the cross has gloriously raised itself, whilst they lie in chains at its feet. 'These crosses, your honour, were never set up here by the hand of man,' said my Paddy, 'but were brought hither from Rome by angels, and stood up of themselves the moment they were laid in the churchyard, and placed themselves in the hole of the pedestal in which your honour sees them standing. The angels had nothing at all to do with it, your honour. The crosses did it, as I said, of themselves. The cross of the holy Columb Kill only has been set up by men.'

Columb Kill, called also Columba, is one of the most celebrated of the Irish saints. He was, as is said of most Irish saints, of royal lineage; for on his father's side he was descended from Nial, who was the father of many kings; while his mother, Aethena, was of the princely house of Leinster. Before she bore her afterwards so celebrated son, she had a dream which I will here narrate, partly in proof of the great celebrity of this saint, partly to give my readers a sample of the fantastic nature of Irish dreams. Adamnan, an Irish author, who wrote so early as the seventh century, relates this dream thus: — 'There appeared to the princess Aethena, as she lay awake one night shortly before her delivery, an angel from heaven, who brought her a veil of wonderful beauty, on which were embroidered and painted the most charming flowers in the entire world. Aethena was astonished at the beauty of the flowers, and wished to catch hold of the veil; but the angel lifted it up, and spread it out; and, when the princess asked him why he so soon deprived her of the present he had displayed to her, he made answer, that this veil was a type of a great and honourable gift she would receive, which likewise she could not retain long for herself, but would be obliged soon to send out into the world. The princess then saw the veil ascend into the air, and spreading itself out wider and wider, slowly depart from her. At last she beheld it, covered with beautiful flowers and glittering stars, spread itself far away over the valleys, mountains, plains, and forests.'

Shortly after she bore Columba, or, as he was at first called, Crimthan, for the name of Columba was afterwards given to him when the dove-like simplicity and innocence of his character became known. Kill, as we have already remarked, means, in ancient Irish, the same as church; so that Columb Kill signifies 'the dove of the church.' Not merely were his labours confined to Ireland, where he founded monasteries and schools, but he was of the greatest importance to Scotland also, whither he emigrated, and whose great apostle he became. The cross which was here raised in his honour, among the ruins of Monasterboice, once fell down and was broken, but has been again set up in its present mutilated condition. At its foot, which stands in a square hole in the pedestal, some water had collected. My Paddy assured me that this water remained here the whole year, and never dried up, even though rain should not have fallen for a long time. People come from far and wide to wash their diseased limbs with this 'sweat of Columba's cross.' They also scrape and scratch off the moss which grows on the surface of the cross, wrap it carefully in paper, take it home, and, 'for good luck,' mix it in their tea.

Has it ever been the custom, any where else in Christendom, to erect large handsome crosses, near churches, to particular saints, as chapels are built, in order there to pray for them? or is this also a custom peculiar to the Irish Christians alone?

I returned on foot to the little hut on the rising ground, where we had left our car, and, as another heavy shower of hail was pouring down on the ruins and the dark fields, I was compelled, for the sake of shelter, more closely to inspect the interior of the cabin. Here I particularly observed the mode of preparation of these oaten cakes which I had seen carved in stone on the cross of St. Patrick, and which form so conspicuous a feature in the whole domestic economy of the north of Ireland and Scotland. These famous oat-cakes are made of coarsely ground oats, the principal grain of Ireland and Scotland, in the following extremely simple and even rude manner. The meal is formed into a thick paste with water, and spread upon a warm circular plate of iron (called a griddle), which is found in every Irish cabin, and is heated by a few handfuls of lighted straw. The paste is spread out on this like a thin pancake, and in a few moments is fit to eat, and dry like biscuit. As the people call this cake, and as they eat these oat-cakes every day, it might lead one to suppose, that, as cake-eaters, the Irish and Scotch live very luxuriously. These cakes, however, taste not much better than flour mixed with water, and afterwards dried. Nevertheless, many persons are passionately fond of them; and the Irish usually assure the stranger, when they show him their oat-cakes, that they are exceedingly wholesome, strengthening, and nourishing, which can only be true of them when compared with the watery and unnutritious potato. The English, who are generally very inquisitive about our black bread — the word *black*[1] horrifies them — and often maliciously remark that such food would not be given even to horses in their country, completely forget that, in Germany, oats are given to horses, and that many millions of inhabitants of their empire would think themselves fortunate in the extreme if they could only get this black bread, and that the Irish call this dried paste *cake*, and consider it the most nourishing food they can procure. All through Scotland and Ireland, particularly in the north, as well as in the north of England, oat-cakes are at home, and he who is fond of them may enjoy them even in London.

The Irish harp, too, which I had seen in the picture of Paradise on the stone cross at Monasterboice, I again found during my sojourn at Drogheda. It was at the house of a Roman Catholic priest, who gave us an Irish musical-poetical soirée, which I reckon one of the most agreeable soirées I ever attended. The reception room of this gentleman, like that of many Irish patriots, was adorned with portraits of Father Mathew, of Moore, and of O'Connell. The latter I scarcely recognised, for he was painted in various colours, with a mantle trimmed with fur, and had his lord mayor's golden chain around his neck. He looked like an old Irish king. Besides these, there were pictures of two celebrated Irish landscapes and ruins, and portraits of some Irish saints and apostles. In one picture was Father Mathew in the open air, on a grassy mound. Behind him, in the dark background, stood a Christian cross, and through the cloudy sky a stream

---

[1] We have 'black bears,' 'black ink,' 'black night,' — but 'black bread' — Mein Gott! it is dreadful! [original footnote].

of light poured down upon it. Before him kneeled and stood the lame, the blind, and the healthy, to whom he was preaching. This picture was interesting to me, as an illustration of the opinions which the Irish entertain of this remarkable man.

Drogheda is a very Irish town — the last genuine Irish one the traveller meets with on this coast as he advances northwards; for, after it, every thing is more inclined to the Scotch. Nay, Drogheda is perhaps more Irish than many a town in the south or west of the island. The population is almost entirely Roman Catholic, and but very few Protestants are to be found there. Drogheda is therefore one of the greatest strongholds of O'Connell, and was much eulogized by him in the speech I heard at Dublin. The *Drogheda Argus*, a large paper published here, contains, in almost every number, some out-and-out repeal-articles, the subject of which is the necessity of a renewed organization of the repeal agitation, and the 'struggle for a national existence.' The suburbs of Drogheda are genuinely Irish, miserable, filthy, falling cabins; and many persons are likewise to be found in the neighbourhood, who understand and speak the old Irish language, and say that they cannot speak English with comfort and fluency. Nay, according to what I was told by the inhabitants, I must believe that the Irish language is far more general in and about Drogheda than at any other point of the eastern coast of Ireland.

As I was now about to take leave of the old Celtic soil, all these matters combined to render me more desirous to be present at such an Irish poetical-musical soirée.

The first person who came forward was an Irish declaimer, a man from among the people, — I know not whether a gardener, a carpenter, a ploughman, or a 'broken farmer,[1]' but I was told he knew a countless number of old Irish poems and songs. He came in and thus addressed me: — 'Out of friendship for him (meaning the priest) I am come: he told me that there was a foreigner here, who wished to hear some of our old Irish poems, and I will gladly recite to him what I know.'

---

[1] The broken farmers very often turn story-tellers in Ireland, [original footnote].

'I am much obliged to you,' said the priest; 'but if you were to recite all you know, we would be obliged to listen to you all night, and perhaps many other nights besides.'

'It is true our forefathers have handed down to us a great number of poems from generation to generation; and very beautiful ones they are too, sir, if you could only understand them. How beautiful is not the song of *Tober a Jollish*, that is, of the glittering spring, which is but three miles distant from our town; or that of *Cuchullin*, the Irish champion, who went to Scotland. Shall I begin with the song of Cuchullin, your reverence?' 'Do, my son, and God bless thee!'

The man began to declaim, and recited for a quarter of an hour without once stopping. The subject of his poem was as follows: Cuchullin was an Irish youth, of princely blood, who went to Scotland to perfect himself in the use of arms. As from all quarters people resorted to Ireland to complete their spiritual, religious, and scientific education, so the Irish youth used to go over to Scotland to practise the arts of arms. In Scotland, Cuchullin fell in love with the daughter of his teacher, Conlear, and swore eternal fidelity to her. But when he returned to Ireland, after completing his studies, and took up his residence at his father's court, occupied in the contentions and battles of his fatherland, he grew up to be a great, mighty, and distinguished man, and forgot his Scottish mistress, who, her love being now turned into hatred and contempt, meditated revenge for the insult offered her. She bore a son, the fruit of the hypocritical love of Cuchullin. This son she had instructed in the use of arms, and all things necessary for a hero: she chose him as the instrument of her revenge, while at the same time, as a memento of Cuchullin, he became an object of her hatred. When Connell, — if I mistake not, this was the name of her son, — had grown up to man's estate, she sent him over to Ireland, commanding him to seek out the far-famed Irish hero Cuchullin, (whom she had taught him to envy and to hate,) to challenge him to fight, to humble, to conquer, and to slay him. That he might do this the more surely, she put him under enchantment, so that, even against his will, he would be obliged to deprive his father of his life. Connell landed in Ireland, and at last, after many chances and adventures, met his father, the great champion Cuchullin, on the battle-field. Connell too was a great Scottish hero, and both were long known to each other by fame; besides, it was customary for the Irish and Scottish heroes to envy, to seek each other, and to fight. On account of their nationality, on account of their fame, and on account of the personal and special enmity and declaration of war on the part of Connell, they were both the bitterest foes. They were only ignorant how closely they were connected by blood. Their combat was long and obstinate. Connell, indeed, the moment he saw Cuchullin rushing towards him on his proud steed, felt himself seized with a strange, melancholy, and, to him, inexplicable, feeling. This sadness and this sympathy, by which he felt himself drawn to his enemy, became still greater when they engaged hand to hand. When he came so near him as to be able to look into his eye, he was seized with a strong foreboding that he to whom he stood opposed, with the murderous sword in his hand, was his long-sought, long-lamented father, over whose existence so impenetrable a mystery had prevailed from his earliest childhood, — whom he so often, according to his mother's account, had believed to be dead, and of whose existence he again at times used to hear something. He fought against his inclination, he parried the blows of his father, he shunned the fight, he wished to throw away his arms, and to save his body and soul by flight. But then again the enchantment his mother had laid him under, seized him with all its power. He pressed again to the combat; with fury, as if impelled by evil spirits, he attacked his father. His soul struggled and resisted in vain; and while he drove his sword, guided by unseen powers, through his father's breast, his own heart broke in the dreadful struggle. Both fell at the same moment from their horses beside each other: the one slain by the weapon of his son, the other thrown to the ground by the excessive agony of his soul. Connell grasped the hand of his dying father; while the revengeful spirit of the enchantress Aithuna hovered exulting over the scene of blood. All now became clear to Cuchullin, while the night of death darkened around him, and his eye-strings brake.

I, or course, did not understand a single word of all this recitation, but my host was kind enough to relate the story to me afterwards. To understand, however, was not so much my object as to convince myself, by my own ears, that this old Ossianic poetry is still living and extant here in Ireland among the people. The reciter was, as I have said, a simple man, and his recitation was as simple, unadorned, and undeclamatory as himself. Sometimes, however, when carried away by the beauty of the poetry and the ideas, he became animated, and even appeared much affected: he would then look at his hearers, as if he expected their sympathy and admiration for himself and his poem. Sometimes I remarked that the metre of the poem changed; and I was told that this was the case in all their poems, and that the metre always adapted itself to the subject. On the battle-field, the father and the son had a dialogue, which they said was the most beautiful part of the whole poem; but that they could give me no idea of it, for when translated into prose it would lose all its sublimity; and that I, being unacquainted with the language, could form as little idea of it through the medium of any other language as a blind man of the splendour of the sun.

After this he recited a *Song of the Fairy Mounts*. The subject was a story often and every where repeated in Ireland, of a fairy queen who finds a youth sleeping on a mountain, falls in love with him, and invites him to go with her, while she tells him of her power and greatness, and the splendour of her fairy palace. He is at last persuaded to do so, but on the condition, that, when he dies, he shall be brought home and buried with his own people. The queen grants this, and takes him away with her. This story reminded me of Goethe's *Erl-King*[1], and of many similar Hungarian and Russian legends. I once thought that the story of the *Erl-King* had sprung from the German mind, but now I would no longer venture to define the circle to which this legend is limited. It seems to me to have gone from the west of Ireland into the very depths of Asia. Even in the legends of the Greeks there is something similar, — the abduction of Ganymede by Jupiter's eagle, and the residence of many other mortals with the Gods.

This reciter told me that most of what he knew was very ancient, and was chiefly Ossianic poetry, of which there was a great deal here in Drogheda, among the people. I had already heard this, and I afterwards heard it repeated at other places in the north. The county of Donegal, in particular, was described to me as full of still living Ossianic poetry. From what I have learned in Ireland, I am much inclined to believe, what others have already asserted, that Macpherson[2] borrowed the materials for his so-called *Poems of Ossian* from manuscripts and popular traditions in the north of Ireland. So much is certain, that a cursory but observant traveller will perceive more indications of Ossianic poetry in Ireland, than an equally cursory and equally observant traveller in Scotland. The whole Irish people, as well the

---

[1] *Erlkönig*, Erle meaning 'alder tree' in English. [Clachan ed.].

[2] James Macpherson (1736 –1796) was a Scottish writer and poet who translated the Ossian cycle of poems.

old Irish in the west as the Saxon-Irish in the east, are far more imbued with a poetic spirit than the people of Scotland, including both the Saxon in the Lowlands, and the Celtic in the Highlands.

'Oisin,' in pure Celtic Irish pronounced 'Oshin,' was — as is now generally acknowledged, since Macpherson's accounts of him are on all sides declared fictions — no Scot, but an Irishman, as well as his father Fingal, or, as he is properly called, Finn Mac-Cul. 'Finn Mac-Cul, your honour, was in those days just such another as our Irish Wellington in these,' said our old reciter to me. Ossian was, as at least my Irish friends believed, born at Tara, the ancient capital of Ireland, where he spent the greater part of his life. As between the Irish and Scotch every thing becomes a subject of controversy, they have also mutually quarrelled about their heroes, as well as about their missionaries and saints. The more cunning, and, in the field of literature, more active Scotch, have adorned themselves with many a plume stolen from Ireland. Macpherson was not the only, although he may have been the most talented, and most successful, perverter of Irish poetry.

This poetry was followed by music — music from that instrument of which the Irish poet, Samuel Lover, sings —

Oh! give me one strain
Of that wild harp again,
In melody proudly its own,
Sweet harp of the days that are flown!

The harp was produced, and a blind young harper prepared to play some old Irish pieces. I was told, that he was one of the most distinguished harp-players in the surrounding country; and, in fact, his music enraptured us all. The first piece he played was *Brian Boru's March*, at the famous battle of Clontarf, on the bay of Dublin. The Irish king Brian Boru, who had made himself sovereign of all Ireland, overcame the Danes at this great battle, in 1014. He himself, however, was slain, shortly after the battle, by the Danish leader Bruadair; and thus Ireland gained a great victory, and lost her greatest monarch. The music of this march is therefore powerful and wild, and at the same time melancholy. It is at once a song of triumph and of mourning. The rapid changes, and the wild beauty of the air, was so great that I believe, if the people had not been in the habit of marching to this music for more than 800 years, it would now place itself by the side of the *Marseillaise*, the *Rakotzy*, and other famous marches. While the Irish listen to these old airs, and think of these old deeds, and while their hearts beat at the recollection of their former glory, their present slavery rises up before them; and they perhaps look forward into a free and glorious future, with the same feelings as they look back towards a once glorious past:

But, Isle of the West,
Raise thy emerald crest,
Songs of triumph shall yet ring for thee.

So sings Lover.

After Brian Boru's march followed the air of *The Fairy Queen*, a very old Irish piece, as I was told. This much I can say, that it was quite a charming composition, — so soft, so enchanting, and so wild, sportive, and playful withal, that during its performance I could think of nothing but the dancing of fairies and the singing of elves. I afterwards heard it several times on the piano, but on that instrument the music was far from being so soft and rich as from the harp of this blind young minstrel. Although this second part of our evening's entertainment, which was given in a language universally intelligible, afforded me much more enjoyment than the first, I am less able to describe it; since, of all the arts, music is that of whose beautiful productions the aesthetic critic is least able to convey an adequate idea by description or criticism.

We were perfectly satisfied with our harper, for he was, in fact, a finished artist; there are, however, others still more exquisite and more famed in Ireland. There is, for instance, a very distinguished harper in the county of Londonderry, of the name of Hempson, a blind man; and another, still more celebrated, named Byrne, whom I often heard mentioned, is, if I mistake not, also blind. The latter, I was told, was generally thought superior to all others. When, therefore, Moore mournfully sings —

The harp that once through Tara's halls
The soul of music shed,
Now hangs as mute on Tara's walls,
As if that soul were dead —

we must not understand him literally. Many harps still thrill all through Ireland; and although the Harper's Society of Belfast was lately dissolved, yet another has been founded at Drogheda, of which the clergyman, whose guest I was for a long time, is the soul and president. His whole room was full of harps, and comprised many new ones which had been made by his directions. With this society a harper's school is connected, in which are sixteen pupils. It was in contemplation to give a concert the following week, at which seven harpers, mostly blind, were to play together. Unfortunately it was not in my power to be present at this assembly of bards. The greatest assemblies of bards used to take place in times of old, in those 'Tara's halls' of which Moore sings.

This Tara, which no Irishman can forbear mentioning, and whose name resounds hundreds and thousands of times every day, in the conversation and in the poems of the Irish, is a little town in the county of Meath, a few miles from Drogheda, not far from the Hill of New Grange. It was once the seat of government, or capital, and was almost in Ireland what Scone Abbey was in Scotland. There stood here a hall or palace, in which the heathen Irish kings and chieftains used to meet, probably at very different times and for very different purposes, but yet regularly every three years, to consult on matters of general importance.

Ollam Fodhla[1] is said to have instituted this triennial national assembly two hundred years before Christ. There the bards also attended; and not only the laws enacted there, but also all important events that occurred in the country, were recorded by them in a great national register, called the Psalter of Tara. Besides, on festive occasions, the bards used there to sing, at the banquets, the history of the country and the deeds of the kings. Even the laws were written in verse, and set to music. This place is now universally called Tara; in the old Irish it was called properly Teamar, or, as my friend said, Taimara, that is, 'the great house.'

The last national assembly held at Tara was in the year 554, *A.D.* in the reign of King Diarmid. This was at the time when Christianity and the Christian priesthood had already become powerful in Ireland. The old heathen institutions and monuments, and the heathen order of bards, who, like the Ulemas of Turkey, and like their own priests, the Druids, had formed a powerful and privileged class, declined and were thrust aside. When a criminal was once dragged from a monastery where he had taken refuge, and punished with death in Tara, the monks loudly denounced it as

---

[1] Ard Ollam or Chief Ollam of Ireland, a position of equal standing to the High King of Ireland.

---

sacrilege, and marching in solemn procession to the palace, pronounced a curse upon its walls. From that day no king sat in Tara; and the monastery which had dared to pronounce a curse upon the most ancient and most celebrated residence of the Irish kings, has since been called 'the Convent of the Curse.'

As the old Druidical palaces and monuments fell into decay on the introduction of Christianity, so did the oldest Irish Christianity and its monuments on the subsequent introduction of Romanism; and so, likewise, did the Roman Catholic churches and institutions wear away in the presence of Protestantism. Catholicism is now zealously striving again to raise itself. Should it succeed in this, then the independent Irish Christianity may again work itself forth from under the domination of Roman Catholicism, and separate from Italy. Druidism and bardism alone are buried irrestorably beneath the ruins of centuries, and can scarcely be born again.

My Irish friend assured me, that it is a peculiarity of the old Irish language, that it has no jargon or vulgar dialect. Every one, even the lowest and most ignorant, speaks it as purely and grammatically as the best Irish scholar. With the English language this cannot be the case; because this Norman-Saxon mixture has been forced upon a number of subjugated and conquered races. The Irish, the Welsh, the Cornish, the Highlanders of Scotland, all must learn English and speak it with their own peculiar dialect. The English dialects are therefore of quite a different character from our German dialects. They are nothing more than corruptions and perversions of a language in the mouths of foreigners; whilst our German dialects are original offshoots of the same language, each of which had, and still has, its own organic life, its own literature and popular poetry, its own strength and beauty.

One of the company assured me that he possessed hundreds of beautiful old songs and poems in manuscript, which had long been hereditary in his family, and not a single one of which had ever been printed. He, like all Irishmen with whom one speaks on this subject, was of opinion that the specimen of old Irish or Ossianic poetry which Macpherson has given us, is partly a very perverted, and partly a very insufficient one, and that his poems give no correct idea of the great beauty and the extraordinary richness of the national well-springs from which they were drawn. I believe all this quite readily; nay, it is more than probable: but then the question presents itself — why does not some genuine, sincere, and truth-loving Irish Macpherson arise, to collect these beautiful emanations of Irish poesy, and translate them into one of the well-known European languages, in order in this way to save at least whatever can be saved of them in another language? The manuscripts, carefully as families preserve them as precious heir-looms, are daily becoming less numerous. The memory of the people, faithful and strong as it may be, without doubt loses every year more and more of the beautiful old verses. And besides, the number of those who can value these verses, enjoy, and learn them, is visibly growing smaller; for the English language is spreading with strides ever increasing in rapidity, while the Irish is retiring before it into the more remote wilds.

The Irish continually assert that their poems are untranslatable, and that all their beauty would be destroyed by translation, — just as a beautiful flower would lose its distinctive character by being painted a different colour. It is, no doubt, difficult to transfer all the fragrance of poetry that lies in verses and words into another language; but Macpherson has shown how the world can be delighted with an imitation, which yet retains much of the original. They should be at least collected and printed in the Irish language.

Social pleasures, such as those with which my Irish friends adorned our evening, are the most delightful which a traveller can enjoy. In by-gone times they were much the custom, but have now long died away. Our pleasures of more recent invention are also here, in this part of the world, on the decrease, partly no doubt to the delight of the friends of intellectual refinement and cultivation. Thus, public balls are everyday becoming more and more out of fashion. The *race balls* are almost the only ones now known; and a quadrille, to the simple music of the pianoforte, satisfies all. In like manner, cards are getting more and more into disuse. No longer than ten years ago, a card-table was regularly provided for the company; but now cards are almost entirely confined to the common people. These are really remarkable, and, at least as to cards, pretty general phenomena throughout Europe. Conversation is every where taking the place of card-playing, so destructive both to mind and pleasure; and should an historian ever write the history of their extension and decline, they can never be sufficiently chastised by him.

From Drogheda to Belfast

School of the Moravian Brethren—'A Noble Pursuit'—Decline of the Noble Pursuit—Stage-Coach Horses—Irish Climate—The County of Louth—Irish Tinkers—Contrasts—Ulster and Cromwell—Borders of Ulster—Erin's Intercourse with Albion—Newry—Flax and Linen Trade—Advantages of the Linen Trade—Contest Between the Irish and English Linen Manufactures—Little Northern Towns—Arrival at Belfast

My kind friend in Drogheda, to whom I am indebted for most of what I saw there, was the proprietor of an excellent private school, which I took an opportunity of visiting. The same friend told me of another distinguished school, which was founded at Grace Hill, not far from Drogheda, by the Moravian Brethren, and is said to be one of the largest and best establishments of the kind in Ireland. Unfortunately I had no time to devote any attention to this interesting institution; and on the following day I took my usual seat on a stage-coach—namely, an outside one, beside the coachman.

This place beside the coachman is always the most comfortable, and consequently the most sought after, of all outside places on English coaches, the coachman being a much more important personage than a passenger, and, of course, far better taken care of. Besides, it is generally provided with a cushion, while the other outside places are only bare wooden benches. Then the coachman has a leather apron, which he buckles before him as a protection against rain and cold, and usually shares with the passenger beside him. The other outside passengers may put their legs in their pockets, to keep them from the rain, if they have not brought leather aprons of their own. And then there are the four spirited and beautiful English horses always before you, the sight of which alone affords great pleasure; and, lastly, there is the coachman beside you, who knows every thing along the road, and every one who resides there, as well as his right hand, since he has probably driven backwards and forwards on this road some thousands of times. Then, should he happen to be silent, which is seldom the case, and not very communicative to the inquisitive stranger, the latter may make the coachman himself the object of his attention and observation.

The trade or art of horse-driving is, in the eyes of the English, one of the noblest of arts, and most worthy of a man,—'a very noble pursuit,' as an

Englishman said to me. Should an English Homer ever write an *Iliad*, the charioteers of his heroes will play a far more important part in it than those of the Grecian Homer. The charioteers of Hector and Achilles but rarely join in the contests of their masters, and punctually fulfill their commands; while the English 'driver' sits on his box so broad and commanding, and behaves with so dignified and lordly an air towards his outside passengers, all of whom are doubtless heroes, that it looks as if he were the chief of the great hero-laden carriage. The public holds in no small estimation the man who can drive four horses with such dexterity, ease, and art: therefore it is, that very respectable and comfortable fellows devote themselves to the exercise of this, the nation's favourite pursuit. As he is very well paid, and is able to lay by no small sums out of the many and good fees which he receives from the passengers, he is generally very respectably dressed, usually enveloped from head to foot in a light-coloured waterproof top-coat, closely buttoned up, and never without white gloves. The reins are handed up to him by the stable boys, and he demands his fee from the passengers in quite a gentlemanly manner. It has even happened that persons, who were neither compelled to do so by birth nor by their pecuniary circumstances, have devoted themselves to the stage-coach, through mere passion for the noble pursuit of driving horses. A lord is said not to have been ashamed to receive his sixpence reward for many years on a public coach. Every thing belonging to his business the coachman understands most perfectly, and all his proceedings go on with a regularity which is astonishing, and unequalled in any other country. The four horses are always of the very best quality, the harness is of the simplest construction, and in the finest order. To see the entire equipage rattle away with this unsurpassable punctuality and quickness, as if winged and animated with reason and reflection by the two hands of the coachman, whose motions are imperceptible, though certain and sure, affords an inexhaustible source of pleasure to the outside passenger, and will make him join and sympathise with the driver, and all friends of the 'noble pursuit,' in their lamentations over the present decline of this art, and every thing connected with it.

Since the construction of railways the famous 'crack coaches' have vanished. As opposition is no longer so great, nor coaches so numerous, fame is no longer to be derived from the pursuit; consequently, few lords will in future be found to rival the coachmen. The occupation is losing its honourable character, and persons of an inferior grade are devoting themselves to it: in a word, the whole art is on the decline, nay, is already fallen, and deeply affecting are the lamentations of all admirers and partisans of the old state of things. In Ireland, however, this is less the case than in England, because Ireland as yet possesses but few miles of railway; and here, therefore, with the improvements of the roads, and the increase of internal traffic, stage-coaches are becoming more numerous. I do not, however, wish it to be understood that the arrangements of the Irish coaches are so perfect as those of England, even though the latter are on the decline.

The friends of animals, and the foes of cruelty to animals, will rejoice at the progress of railways, for to them the rapid driving of the English coachmen, who treated their horses as mere machines, was a revolting cruelty. According to one system, it was, and still is, considered most advantageous to drive the horses for five years; according to another it is deemed better to drive them for four years only; that is, those who adopt the former think that it is more to their interest to feed the horses well, and work them so little as to make them last for five years; whilst the advocates of the latter system consider it more profitable to feed a horse with a diet barely sufficient, and to subject him to such excessive work and speed that he will be knocked up after three or four years, when he is declared useless, and either killed, or harnessed to a cart.

The driver with whom I deposited myself at Drogheda, was, unfortunately, of a very taciturn and morose nature, and I was left altogether to these reflections on English coachmen, and to my own observation of the country through which we were passing. He did not even offer me (what properly and of right belongs to the box-passenger, who usually pays something more for the advantages he enjoys,) half of his apron, to protect me against the *extremely temperate* climate of Ireland, which alternately greeted us with rain, hail, and snow, intermixed with wind and occasional glimpses of sunshine, in order the better to dry us again. For the linen bleach-grounds, in the north of Ireland, this species of mild climate must be very welcome; but we found it not at all agreeable that our linen should be subjected to this bleaching process on our own bodies. One cannot help remarking, when he hears so much of the extraordinary mildness of the Irish climate, that to man it is of extremely little advantage. To the arbutus, the ivy, and other plants, it may be very beneficial; but man desires something more than such a mixture of sunshine and cold rain,— of a tepid and moist cold atmosphere all through the year, notwithstanding the thermometer may declare it mild and temperate. To be regularly warm once in the year, one would willingly submit to be once cold also; but to be frozen the whole year through, in summer as well as in winter, will seem an advantage to no one.

Drogheda is surrounded on every side by a group of little mountains; then follows a plain; then, again, another little group of mountains, near Newry and Dundalk, followed by another plain at Belfast, which, in its turn, is succeeded by more mountains. Thus the surface of the country alternates in Ireland. The first plain between Drogheda and Dundalk is the county of Louth, the appearance of which affords but little pleasure. It is the most extreme county of the province of Leinster, towards the north, and seems to have participated least of all in the English improvements introduced into Leinster. Every thing is here so wretchedly Irish, the cabins of the people are so miserable, the appearance of the cultivated land so wild, the inhabitants so poor and ragged, as is usually seen only in the most remote western parts of Erin. Nay, it almost seems to become worse the nearer one approaches the confines of Leinster. To this, Dundalk, a clean town, very picturesquely situated on a little bay that runs far into the land, is the only exception; but the hills and mountains which succeed it resemble in appearance true hills of misery, and reminded me of the Hungry Hills in Kerry. The aspect of these bare hills is perfectly wild and uncomfortable. Excepting the fine level road, scarce a trace of the arranging, creating hand of man is to be seen; for the cabins, which stick to the hills like swallows nests, bear little resemblance to a work of man.

I dismounted from the coach as we were going up the hills; and, while the coachman was doing something to the coach, I took a look at some of these miserable habitations. Before one of them I found an Irish tinker, employed in mending a potato-pot. A great hole had been burnt in it, so near the bottom that it could never have been entirely filled. I asked the peasant woman, who was looking on, how long the kettle had been in this unpatched broken condition. 'Many a long year, your honour,' replied she; 'for the last couple of years, when I boiled the potatoes, I had always to put it a little on one side on the fire, so that the water could not reach the hole. The tinkers do not often come here; and when they do, they charge so dear for every little job, that we have been obliged to do without them.'

The tinkers in Ireland, as every where else, are a nomadic class, but here of course they are covered with rags from head to foot. 'The tinkers are rovers,' was always the remark of the Irish to me; 'that is, they are constantly rambling about.' The tinkers usually ramble about only in the fine season, and often with their families, like our gipsies. In the winter they dwell mostly in little mud-cabins, on some great bog, where they can get fuel cheap or for nothing. Sometimes these mud-cabins stand for several years; but sometimes they are built merely for the severe season, and the next year others are required.

On the other side of this miserable range of hills—the inhabitants of which are for years looking forward for the time when they can resolve to get the potato-pot, the principal and most important piece of furniture in an Irish cabin, mended—is the boundary line of the provinces of Ulster and Leinster. The coach rolled over it; and scarcely had it done so than we seemed to find ourselves in a different world. As with the stroke of a magician's wand—the expression is not a whit too strong—the filthy cabins by the wayside were changed into habitable, yes, pretty houses, painted with various colours. Regular plantations, well-cultivated fields, even little gardens, and trees planted in rows, met the eye right and left. At first I would not trust my eyes, and imagined it was all an illusion, or that the change was perhaps only transient, and confined to the property of some individual landlord favourable to improvement; but it continued to Newry, and, beyond it again, the whole way to Belfast. I now saw that quite a different state of things prevailed here, and that at the boundary the physiognomy of Ulster, the land of the Scottish colonists, the industrious Presbyterians, had actually turned itself towards me.

Of course the entire province of Ulster, or the north of Ireland, does not present this prosperous appearance; nor is it inhabited wholly by Scotch colonists and Presbyterians. On the contrary, many districts of it, as I will hereafter show, are inhabited by genuine Celtic-Irish. In those portions there are whole tracts as wild as any other part of Erin; for instance, the great mountain county of Donegal, and, generally, most of the mountainous parts of Ulster; but just here, at the boundary, the contrast between the two provinces is as striking as I have described above. It seems as if every thing Irish and miserable had been driven from Leinster to her mountainous borders; and as if Ulster, on the contrary, had pushed out her best colonists here to the feet of the mountains. With a sigh the traveller takes leave of old Ireland, and with a shout of triumph Presbyterian Ireland receives him.

I have read the narratives of many travellers who crossed the boundary line of Ulster and the southern provinces at other points, and have invariably found that, as soon as they entered Ulster, even although they were not aware of having passed the boundary, they all remark the great improvement in the appearance and cultivation of the country. It seems that this line of contrast and boundary runs from sea to sea, from the bay of Newry to the bay of Donegal. I explain this phenomenon in the following manner: It is well known that since the conquest of Ireland, nearly 700 years ago, the English have done all in their power to destroy, or at least completely to Anglicize, the ancient Celtic race, and, at various times, have made use of various means, both peaceful and warlike, to accomplish their design. Persuasion, education, proselytism; then, again, force, war, punishment, death, banishment;—all have been employed for this purpose. Once they attempted to root out the entire Irish people at one fell swoop,—to destroy this curse-laden people like rats, to drive them into the sea, to pack them in ships, and thus banish or transport them to foreign lands. Then, again, they endeavoured, by persuasion, by force, by all kinds of disadvantageous laws, to lead the people away from their language, their national costume, their religion, and in all these points gradually to Anglicize them. All the persecutions which the English have for 700 years employed, lawfully and unlawfully, against the Irish, against their national dresses and education, against their right to property, against their language, against their church, against their antiquities, fill in English history some volumes, which are written in blood, and over which an Irishman might sing Jeremiads no less affecting and saddening than the lamentations of the Jewish prophet[1].

The English, and especially the Scotch Presbyterians, and, above all, their hero Cromwell, resolved to clear the province of Ulster entirely of the Irish. As Cromwell saw that it was not possible completely to root out all the

---

[1] Thomas Moore does this in his poem entitled *The Parallel*, composed on reading a treatise by a Mr. Hamilton, in which he endeavoured to that the Irish were originally Jews:— Like them doth our nation lie conquer'd and broken, And fall'n from her head is the once royal crown; In her streets, in her halls, desolation has spoken, And while it is day yet, her sun has gone down! [original footnote].

Irish at once, he determined to have Ulster at least for himself and his colonists, and to drive the Irish from it as far as possible into the west of Connaught. Without more ado, these poor people were forced, with bag and baggage, from their soil across the borders of Ulster; whilst the Scotch came over from the Lowlands by thousands, and took possession of the land, to which they had as little right as the pickpocket to the watch he niches. This process of banishment of the old population, and the new colonization of Ulster, must naturally have produced greater consequences on its borders; for there the expulsion was more easily effected, and there it was most important to settle new Scotch colonists. The poor expelled inhabitants naturally preferred settling in the neighbourhood of their old abodes; because, the further they went, the greater opposition would they meet from the older possessors. Thus it may be explained why, near the boundaries, the contrasts of the two races are even to the present day greatest and most striking.

Nor was it under Cromwell alone that these expulsions, confiscations, grants, and new colonizations took place in Ulster. Long before his time, they were had recourse to in the reigns of various English kings; and were repeated also after him, by William III., after the battle of the Boyne. Ulster is that part of Ireland which inclines most to Scotland, and approaches so near it, that at all times one may pass from one country to the other in a few hours. This is the point at which Great Britain and Ireland almost touch; whilst toward the south they diverge from each other. While, therefore, for a long period there was no connection between the history of the south of Ireland and that of the south of Great Britain, the histories of the north of Ireland, or Ulster, and of the north of Great Britain, or Scotland, were long interwoven with one another. The population of these two districts were probably, from very remote times, alternately at peace and war with each other, and both without doubt, in the very earliest times, interchanged their inhabitants. The inhabitants of Erin frequently passed over to assist the Picts against the Romans, or to seek plunder on the coasts; and in like manner the inhabitants of Albion (the old Celtic name of Scotland) often came over to Erin, either to wage war with the Irish themselves, or to assist native warriors in their contests.

From the fusion of the histories of Northern Ireland and southern Scotland has arisen a confusion of their names. For instance, about the end of the third century, and also in the fourth and fifth, we find that the inhabitants of Erin, as well as those of Albion, were called 'Scots;' while at this time, and for many hundred years after, Ireland was called 'Scotland' par excellence; and Scotland seems at a much later period to have gradually claimed this name for itself. In the middle of the third century, some Irish, calling themselves Scots, crossed over to Albion or Caledonia, under the command of their king, Carbry Riada. The Scottish, that is, Irish king, founded a colony in Argyleshire, by which at last the entire country was Scotticized and called Scotland; while the successors of Carbry Riada became kings of Caledonia, and Ireland gradually lost its name of Scotland, and again assumed its ancient one of Erin, which is concealed in Hibernia, Ireland, and Irland.

Newry is a large and handsome town; that is, it is large among the small, and has a very pleasing appearance. Its houses are prettily built, its streets are ornamented with trees, and its bay is always full of ships. Here begins the real flax, linen, spinning, weaving, and bleaching country; and the further north we go, the finer become the threads and texture of the linen. The little towns of Banbridge and Moyallan especially, are distinguished for their excellent and very fine flax. All these little places—Banbridge, Dromore, Hillsborough, and others which we passed—look clean, prosperous, pretty, and very thriving; and they all look bleached, orderly, and, what they ought to be, like the linen they produce.

This branch of industry is of a very peculiar nature. When flourishing, it is, for numerous reasons, unquestionably one of the most beneficial any country can desire. It gives food and a more healthy employment to a far greater number of hands, and is more conducive to culture and refinement than a multitude of other branches of industry. It is conducive to agriculture, because the flax can be grown in the country, and requires a very attentive cultivator. The cotton and silk trades are of no advantage to agriculture in our northern climates, as they must derive their materials from abroad. The wool trade requires only the rude care of the shepherd, and is less favourable to culture in proportion as the rank of the shepherd is inferior to that of the agriculturist. A flourishing corn trade gives employment to the rough hand of the peasant only. But linen requires a number of little manipulations, which are partly secure from the destructive influence of new machines and inventions. The first treatment to which flax is subjected, and its conversion into a material fit for spinning, will be always left to the peasants, and will scarcely ever fall into the hands of the manufacturers; while cotton is delivered to the machines just as nature supplies it. The spinning of the flax, too, remains much longer in the hands of the labourer and his family. At last, indeed, a flax-spinning machine has been invented, which is ruining the poor spinners. But flax is a much nobler production than cotton, and capable of being carried to much greater perfection. Some of the finest threads therefore can never be spun by machinery, and will always remain in the hands of men. The Brabant spinners of lace yarn fear not the most inventive heads, or the most ingenious machinery in the world. So is it also with the weaving of the linen. On account of its smoothness, its durability, and firmness, flax is capable of being worked with far greater art than cotton. What beautiful damask patterns we see made of flax and silk, but never of cotton! This gives, in the province of the linen manufacture, far more scope for the exercise of talent, and much greater independence, than the cotton manufacture, which can do every thing by machinery, has no need of the hand and intellectual talents of man, but makes mere unskilled slaves of all its labourers. The bleaching of the linen is now, indeed, carried on by rich capitalists, who are possessed of chemical secrets, for which they have patents; but I believe, the best bleached and least injured linen is always obtained from those who make use of the old natural means,—the sun, the rain, and the wind.

Besides, all the manipulations to which the flax and linen are subjected, are of a clean and delicate nature: every thing aims at fineness and whiteness; and this requires a certain delicacy of hand, and refinement of mind, which is unnecessary in other employments, as the herdsman, the field-labourer, or the sailor. It therefore seems that a flourishing linen manufacture must be conducive to the extension of order, cleanliness, and intellectual refinement throughout the country. How pleasing and even poetical is the spectacle of girls employed in bleaching, at their spinning-wheels, and at their looms!

The linen manufacture is, moreover, far less pernicious in a moral point of view than many other branches of trade, which open door and gate to deceit and gambling. We need only call to mind the flour, tea, and corn trades—the adulterators of flour, and the gamblers in corn. So detested a class as the corn-dealers, the linen trade can never produce, nor such a class as the deceitful millers; for the linen lies clear before the eyes of every one, and its fineness or coarseness is capable of no adulteration, though to this there are of course a few exceptions. The rude peasant, the rough thresher, the deceitful miller, the avaricious baker, the hard-hearted corn-dealer, are moral products, which ripen on the boughs and branches of the corn trade. The provident husbandman, the girl singing at her spinning-wheel, the industrious and attentive weaver, the poetic-looking bleaching-maid, the linen-trader, honest against his will,—these are the persons to whom the salutary stream of the linen manufacture gives support, when, divided into many branches, it flows through a land. It is therefore always pleasing to the traveller to arrive in a country that produces flax, yarn, and linen, particularly when the trade is vigorous and flourishing. This is now, indeed, as we have hinted above, no longer the case in Ireland, since the establishment of rival manufactories in England. English speculators have also erected large factories in Belfast; so that at this moment nearly all branches of the manufacture of linen and yarn, even to the bleaching, are passing from the hands of the many poor people, into those of a few great capitalists. The preparation of flax and linen in the north of Ireland has been brought over either by the Scotch settlers, or has flourished here in Ireland, and in the south of Scotland, from ancient times. It is curious that in Scotland, as in Ireland, the south-eastern parts near the sea are the principal seats of this manufacture. In Scotland, Dundee is the chief seat of this trade, as Belfast is in Ireland. Both countries produce, I believe, about equal quantities of linen, but Ireland seems to *export* more. It is impossible, however, to ascertain this point correctly, as the returns of the two countries are not founded on the same principles. The linen manufacture of Scotland is stated to have produced only 1,500,000 yards in the year 1707, whilst it now produces nearly twenty-five times as much. The production of this article has increased in the same ratio in Ireland since 1698, though at the expense of the woollen manufacture, which then flourished in the south of Ireland. This took place in consequence of the battle of the Boyne, which gave Ireland again into the hands of the English. The woollen was the only manufacture which had then made any progress in Ireland: it was confined to the south, and stood greatly in the way of the English woollen manufacture, which began to flourish in the reign of William III.. The English parliament therefore resolved to destroy the Irish manufacture, and passed a bill by which an exorbitant duty, equivalent to a prohibition, was imposed on its exportation; and thus this branch of industry was totally ruined. In order in some measure to remunerate the Irish for this loss, the linen manufacture was encouraged, as it was not feared by the English, who had as yet none of their own; and so long, at least, as the present union of the two countries continues, a repetition of the distinctive prohibitory regulations is not to be feared.

Nearly all the little towns through which we passed that evening were lighted with gas. It is remarkable how this important new invention has already penetrated all through this country. In Germany, only the largest towns can boast of being lighted with gas, and these too only partially. In the United Kingdom, towns lighted with gas can no longer be counted.

At last we arrived at the centre-point of all the present light of the north of Ireland, the centre of all the flax-spinning and linen-weaving,—at the great thick hanks of men and houses which Irish flax has here twisted together—at Belfast. I believed, at first, that some great festival was being celebrated; for, in whatever direction I looked, I saw the great four, five, and six-storied houses illuminated from top to bottom. There were buildings among them from which light flashed from one or two hundred windows at the same time. I had for a moment forgotten that I had arrived in a great manufacturing town, the only one of importance that Ireland possesses.

Belfast and its Linen Manufactories

Extraordinary Increase of Population In Belfast—The Owner of Belfast—The Linen-Hall—Exportation of Linen—Modes of Packing it—The Whims of the Markets—Giving a Dress—Flax-Spinning—The Hand-Loom and The Power-Loom—Varieties of Flax—Spinning By Machinery—The Bleaching Grounds—Rapidity of Bleaching—Chemical Bleaching Preparations—Northern Presbyterianism and Southern Catholicism—Liszt taken for O'Connell—Party-Spirit—Religious Parties—The Presbyterian Church in Ireland—Presbyterian Parties—Unitarians—Junction and Separation of the Presbyterian Synods—Presbyterian Missions—The Home Mission—Irish Preachers—Irish Schools—The Sunday Schools—Art and Science at Belfast—The Museum—Private Collections—The Botanic Garden— Grasses and Exotic Plants—Musical Societies—The Harpers' Society—Fever-Epidemic—Proportion of Fever Patients to their Various Occupations—Proportion of the Fever Patients to the Sexes

Belfast, in the year 1821, contained 37,000 inhabitants, and in 1831, 53,000. In ten years, therefore, its population increased about thirty per cent.,—an increase unequalled in Ireland. The town has also greatly increased during the last ten years, probably in the same proportions as before, and may now contain nearly 73,000 inhabitants. It is remarkable that, as well in its linen trade as its increase of population, Belfast has kept equal pace with Dundee, in Scotland. In 1821, Dundee had 30,000 inhabitants; in 1831, 45,000; and has now over 60,000. The great increase is, in both places, caused by the linen manufacture, by which numbers of the inhabitants of the open country have been induced to become inhabitants of the towns.

This vast mass of human beings, and all the houses they inhabit, live and stand one and all on the ground and soil of one proprietor, the Marquis of Donegal, to whom the entire town belongs, to whom every citizen pays tribute. Two hundred and fifty years ago, it was still very insignificant, and James I. made a present of the barony of Belfast to Sir Arthur Chichester, who had done much to promote the English interests in this country, without having the least idea of the city that would grow up on it for his posterity. From this place the Marquis of Donegal, whose family name is still Chichester, takes his title of Lord Belfast. It is said that the present marquis could derive an annual revenue of £300,000 from the town, had not a former possessor let the ground at trifling rents, and for very long terms. This has, however, been of great advantage to Belfast.

The linen manufacture and the linen trade being the principal staple and support of Belfast, it therefore claims the greatest attention from the traveller. The linen-hall, a large quadrangular building, which was erected at the end of the last century, is the central point of this trade in Belfast. In this building, almost all the linen of the north of Ireland, destined for exportation, is collected, finished, sorted, and 'made up and dressed' for those countries for which it is destined. Every considerable house has here its ware-rooms and stall, and a walk through the hall is therefore very interesting and instructive.

The linen is sent from here to London, to the United States, to British America, to Spain, to the Brazils, and, lately, to China also. For each market there is not only a particular kind of linen which it prefers, but for each there is also a particular mode of packing, and a particular mode of ornamenting the outsides of the packages. London receives the plainest packages: they must have no ornament of any kind, and every decoration of the linen would only awaken in the inhabitants of that city a prejudice against it. On the contrary, they are very particular and extremely nice about the quality of the linen; and London therefore always receives the best qualities in the plainest wrappers. An extensive linen manufacturer, who had the kindness to conduct me through his ware-rooms, told me that his people had once neglected the above rule, and had sent a bale of linen to a London house, each parcel of which bore on it a little ornament; he no longer remembered what the ornament was, but it might probably have been a couple of silver threads drawn through the band that enclosed the piece, or something similar. This immediately brought down a reprimand from the London dealer, who claimed a slight deduction from the price of each piece, on the ground that he had not ventured to offer the pieces thus ornamented to any of his customers until they had been repacked in a different manner. This individual, so sensitive respecting the external decoration of the linen, had at that time a capital of not more than £500; he is now worth £300,000, principally acquired, it is probable, by his accurate knowledge of the humours of his London customers.

The most directly opposed to the London market in this respect, is that of North America, for which the packages can scarcely ever be too highly ornamented. They are tied up with ribbons of various colours, and ornamented with birds, flowers, &c., which stand out prettily from the white linen. A very favourite linen in America is that on which appears a condor tearing a lamb,—a vignette very common in the Belfast linen-hall on linen intended for America. 'American linen must be more dressed,' repeated my friend. Manufactories and ware-rooms give the observer an opportunity of studying the character of distant lands and people.

As the whole of South America is accustomed to German linen, the Belfast speculators studiously give to the fabrics intended for Santa Cruz, Rio Janeiro, Pernambuco, &c., a German dress. They imitate both the German and Swiss linens in their external ornaments. In particular, they make use of the Prussian eagle, which they place with extended wings on all pieces destined for South America, that it may pass for the linen of Silesia or Bielefeld. The South Americans will take no linen on which they do not see this eagle. One of the Belfast linen merchants has procured a very ornamented coat of arms, of an old German family, which he puts on his South American linen. Thus 'every market has its whim,' as my guide expressed himself.

Even to Germany, as to Hamburgh, for instance, considerable bales of linen are sent. I saw a great bale of parcels, all of which had on them a Swiss cottage, surrounded by flowers and birds, and which was destined for Hamburgh. They are sent there in order to be re-exported as genuine German manufacture. This speculation is possible, because as linen is cheaper in Belfast than in Germany, and as it pays no duty at Hamburgh, the transport costs but little; and the South Americans, when they know the linen comes from Hamburgh, and see the Swiss cottages, are satisfied that it is genuine German or Swiss linen they receive. This they do not call cheating, but speculation, or 'giving a dress.' By this imitation of German linen, and also by obtaining labourers from Germany, this northern linen manufacture has greatly increased and improved. From France, also, some peculiar branches of the trade have been introduced. Thus, French or Belgian workmen have settled at Belfast, and there founded the now not insignificant manufacture of cambric. Many French linens also are here imitated; for instance, the Bretagne linens, which, as well as the German, are so much admired in Spain, and go by the name of 'Britannia.'

Among the flax-mills of Belfast, the most important are those of the Messrs. Mulholland, which are far more extensive than the largest establishments of the same kind at Dundee. At Leeds, in England, are the largest and most splendid flax-mills in the United Kingdom, those of Marshall and Co. A linen-weaving establishment is very often established in connection with these flax-mills; and the whole concern is then designated a linen-yarn factory. Within the last forty years, many cotton spinning and weaving factories have also been added; and on the whole, Belfast now numbers twenty-one great 'cotton and linen-yarn factories,' some of which are so vast as to employ 2000 persons, and some of them rise to the imposing height of eight stories. A very considerable quantity of the linen, I believe much more than one-half, is still made in the country by hand-looms; yet 'power-weaving,' as the English call weaving by machinery, is increasing every day. The melancholy and much-felt battle between the hand-loom and the power-loom, which in some towns of England has been decided in favour of the latter, is going on in Belfast.

As the growth of flax in the north of Ireland is insufficient for the supply required by the linen manufacturers, one sees in the great factories of Belfast, flax from all countries of the world, Russia, France, Holland, and even Egypt, all of which is used for various purposes. The largest and the best is brought from Egypt; the longest is the Russian, from Riga; the finest and most valuable is the Dutch. The flax of the county of Down is the most esteemed Irish flax. In some of the mills the flax is now broken by machinery, in what are termed the 'hackling-rooms.' Flax-spinning by machinery was for a long time a matter of great difficulty to thinking heads, because the process to be invented for that purpose should be founded on principles quite different from those of the woollen and cotton-spinning machines, the flax consisting of a number of long smooth fibres, which could not be spun so easily as the short and closely-united threads of cotton and wool. At last it was suggested to pass the flax through warm water: by this means the fibres are divided, and, I believe, somewhat curled and tangled, so that they are easily spun into a continuous thread. By the warm water it was possible to dispense with the twisting and guiding hand of the spinning-girl; and in the great manufactories one girl can now, alas! superintend no less than fifty-four spinning-wheels. Thus all the busy, humming, little spinning-wheels are now melted into great, noisy, gigantic machines; and the many comfortable little rooms that resounded with the songs of the spinners are changed into spacious gas-lighted halls, in which the ruling voice of the inspector commands silence and requires unremitting toil.

The bleaching-girls are no better off than the spinners. Chemistry has now made such vast progress, that it supplies much quicker and more powerful means for the bleaching than the country man has at his command. Avaricious speculation, which seeks to do every thing at the least possible cost, combines a multitude of resources for this purpose, and thus many little establishments are united into one large one. Hence, in the neighbourhood of Belfast, there are several extensive bleaching establishments, or, as they are called, 'Bleaching-grounds,' or 'Linen-greens,' which are usually the property of those gentlemen who have factories in the town. I visited one a few miles from Belfast: it consisted of great factories, of six-storied buildings, in the midst of beautiful meadows, with chemical works, labourers' cottages, and outhouses. The bleaching-grounds of Belfast are said to possess advantages over those of any other town in the United Kingdom. They are situated in a beautiful plain which surrounds Belfast, and lies at the feet of high and rather steep hills. The water, which flows down in abundance from these hills, and is of particular advantage in bleaching, never fails in any part of the year; and for this reason also water is as generally employed as steam, in Belfast, as the moving power for machinery. Belfast bleachers have even been taken over to England and Wales; but still it has been found impossible to attain the pure whiteness of the Belfast linen. The changeful climate of Northern Ireland is probably extremely favourable to the process. The largest chemical factories are near at hand, at Glasgow, and partly too in Belfast itself.

I had scarcely any idea what a manifold and various apparatus of implements, buildings, machines, and chemical preparations, are required for the perfect management of so simple a process as bleaching. The art has been brought to so high a degree of perfection in these Belfast bleaching-grounds, that a large quantity of raw linen can be completely bleached in four and twenty hours. This rapidity is indeed by no means beneficial for the linen; but, under pressing circumstances, it may be sometimes useful to trade and to humanity. If, for instance, by such fires as those of New York or Hamburgh, great quantities of linen are consumed, it is possible, by these rapid processes, to provide the poor sufferers in a very short time with linen fully bleached. By the various processes to which the linen is subjected, the most various effects and tints of colour are produced,—blue-white, pink-white, yellow-white, and chalk-white, according to the colour most in demand with their consumers. I do not know whether this has been carried to such perfection in Germany. The number and greatness of the chemical preparations I found on these bleaching-grounds amazed me. There is the 'wheat-starch,' made in Ireland; the 'bleaching-liquid,' brought from Glasgow and Belfast; the 'blue,' prepared in Liverpool for the entire kingdom; and the vitriol, which is mixed with water in small portions. Then there are the various contrivances for saturating the linen with these compounds, and other machines to wash out these chemical preparations again after every soaking. There are the 'blueing, starching, wringing, and beetling machines,' the last of which serve to give the linen its final gloss. The gloss is also of various kinds: there is the high-finished, the soft-finished, and the German-finished gloss. The Americans know this German gloss, and the Belfast bleachers must therefore attend to it. They also know how to place the beaters, that after the beetling it assumes a watered appearance. Then there are the drying-houses, where it is dried by the wind, or, if the case is urgent, by artificial heat. All these things are here so perfect that they seem to be prepared for every chance and necessity of trade, and to be able to comply with the whims of all the markets in the world.

Many little contrivances are here to be seen for measuring the strength of the different bucks. These scientific contrivances are now more and more exploding the ancient 'rule of thumb,' that is, the old way the bleachers had of trying the strength of the bucking-washes by the tongue, and the taste. Many of the chemical instruments, and nearly all those made of glass, are procured from Germany; as is likewise the case in most of the manufactories of England where chemical apparatus is used.

Damask is now manufactured at Belfast in considerable quantities; and the inhabitants are not a little proud that their factories make damask even for the table of her most gracious Majesty.

Many other branches of trade have also been established at Belfast, especially during the last ten years. Several of these have been introduced by philanthropists, who dreaded, that, if the entire industrial activity, or the entire existence of the population, depended on the linen manufacture alone, great misery might be occasioned by adverse and unexpected changes, and who thus endeavoured to prepare and open the way for a more diversified activity. The growing necessities of the linen trade, which increased in refinement every day, also caused many other branches of industry to spring up and flourish. Thus there are here ironworks, glass manufactories, white lead works, &c., most of which are offshoots from the great mother-factories at Glasgow. The most strange, and, at first sight, to a German, most inexplicable, of these subordinate trades, is that of the philosophical instrument makers, who are found all over England, but the true meaning of whose name I here for the first time discovered. By these are meant the makers of chemical and physical apparatus. The most remarkable fact, however, in the history of Belfast manufacture and art, is that the first printing press was set up in this city so late as in the year 1696: printing was therefore introduced into many Russian towns much earlier than into this British city. Yet Belfast, since the introduction of printing, has, next to Dublin, produced more printed books than any other city in Ireland. Here, in 1714, was printed the first Bible in Ireland; and here the oldest Irish periodical, *The Weekly Magazine*, was established. Germany, therefore, has many older periodicals than Ireland. Seven newspapers are now published in Belfast, all more or less Whiggish, and, like the Roman Catholic papers of the south, not only opposed to the Tories, but also to the Church of England.

In the Irish rebellion, at the close of the last century, the Presbyterians of the north, and the Catholics of the south rose in concert, and at the same time: the former fought no less obstinately against the English troops than the latter, and they received all accounts of the progress of the French Revolution with as much exultation as the Catholics. Like the Catholics, they are favourable to republican, or, at least, to anti-aristocratic and anti-English tendencies. Nevertheless, they are no friends of the southern Catholics, and, under particular circumstances, are their bitterest enemies. O'Connell and his party have less influence in Belfast than in almost any other town in Ireland; and on all the agitation-expeditions and triumph-progresses which this great man makes through Erin's plains and towns, he carefully avoids Belfast. Of course he has some partisans here, whom he once visited; but he arranged it so that he arrived by night, in a mean-looking carriage, and went off again before the opposite party had time to concert and execute any movement against him. I was told at Belfast that the great musician Liszt had the misfortune to be taken for O'Connell in the neighbourhood of that city, and was very near undergoing something extremely disagreeable that was intended for the agitator. As Liszt approached from Newry, in a handsome chaise drawn by four horses, and it was rumoured that the carriage contained a celebrated man, some of the Presbyterian rabble imagined it was O'Connell. They stopped the carriage, cut the traces, and compelled the eminent pianist to dismount, in order that they might wreak their anger against him in Irish fashion. They merely wished to duck him in a neighbouring pond, and then to advise him to return to his carriage, and to be off to the south of Ireland. It was some time before they discovered that, instead of the well-fed, old O'Connell, a young artist had fallen into their hands. It is the peculiar and unfortunate characteristic of Irish parties, that they agree in scarcely a single point, and that their interests and sympathies are so different, that they can unite on no common ground for the good of all. It is true that all who live on the soil of Erin, are one and all Irish in some particular, and must necessarily feel a certain degree of sympathy for their fatherland, which they have either entered as colonists, or inhabited from times of old. The original native Celts, the English and Scotch colonists, the Roman Catholics, the Presbyterians, the High Churchmen, the poor tenants, the merchants, the landed gentry, have become, or have ever been, Irish. The name of Erin finds an echo in the hearts of all, and there is not one among them who does not lament her ill-fortune. They are all, too, in some way opposed to the pretensions of England: the original Celts and Catholics are, of course, the natural enemies of every thing English; the Presbyterians, as well as the Scotch, are opposed to the Established Church. Nay, the Irish Presbyterians have even their separate opposition against the Kirk of Scotland, which, as the mother-church, sometimes attempts to exercise a certain authority over the Irish synod. So, in like manner, the Irish High-Church party is by no means always in harmony with the English Church party; and the interests of the Irish Presbyterian, or Lutheran, or Roman Catholic trades'-people and manufacturers, of Celtic or Saxon origin, have always been clashing with those of England. The Irish nobility, too, by no means hold the same opinions as the English: the Irish nobleman is made the subject of raillery in England, and the English nobleman is no favourite in Ireland. From all this, one might expect that a fine, unanimous, and powerful opposition would have been formed in Ireland against England; and that all parties would at least join hands in patriotic exertions against England. The parties of other countries, as in France, for instance, always unite as soon as their country is threatened from without; and however violent party feuds may be, all are brothers as soon as the enemy appears.

In Ireland, however, it is precisely the reverse. So often as the foe and oppressor, England, appears, so often she is sure to find numbers ready, through party-hate, to suppress a portion of their patriotic sympathies, and even to sacrifice a portion of their own interests, to save the remainder, and to satisfy their hatred. Thus, although the Irish landlords did not like the restrictions to which, before the Union, the trade of Ireland was subjected, and by which they were sufferers, they did not raise their voice against them, because they required the support of the English kings to retain their grants of property. Thus, again, although the Irish parliament did not like to be commanded by that of England, yet it showed itself obedient in order to retain its privileges. Thus, also, the Presbyterians and the Roman Catholics, although both opposed to the Established Church and the Protestant aristocracy, yet hate each other so much the while, that they often desert and betray one another in the midst of the battle. It is said that, in the last rebellion, Presbyterian rebels looked on inactive, and took pleasure in seeing parties of Catholics cut down by the English, although it was against these very Englishmen they were both fighting.

Thus the interests of no two Irish parties run parallel with each other; and even though both are hostile to England, they are still more hostile to one another, and make friends with England half against their own inclination. People think and feel in Ireland so differently on the most important concerns of man, religion, government, nationality, &c., and are all so differently interested in each of these matters, that it is next to impossible to propose or to carry out any general measure which is not considered as poison by some, whilst by others it is received as a healing and refreshing drink. It is proposed to provide workhouses for the destitute: the Presbyterians are well pleased, because they hope to get rid of beggars and disorder; but the Catholics, whose church encourages almsgiving, are averse to it, in order not to be doubly taxed. Is it intended to provide schools for the people: the Protestants insist on the *whole* Bible being used in them; the Catholics, on the contrary, will have *no* Bible at all, and then education and civilization suffers. Is the draining of the bogs taken into consideration, or the cultivation of the barren mountains: the farmers applaud, but the great folks do not wish to lose the pasturage for their sheep; or the landlords applaud, and then the peasantry do not like to lose their turf. Is it intended to lighten the pressure of tithes on the farmers: the Established Church shakes her head, and the Catholic chapels nod encouragement. If people in the west rejoice that something is doing for the Celtic language and literature, and that a professorship of Celtic literature has been lately erected in the university of Dublin, it is made a subject for derision in the east; and the Union, to maintain which one party would die, another would give their lives to destroy. When these differences will cease, and all these prejudices be smoothed down, no one can foresee. At all events, the commencement which has been made proceeds at so slow a rate, that one cannot venture to calculate the distance of the goal. The Celts are but slowly disappearing before the advance of the Saxons, and a difference of language will long exist. The Catholics have still so much to demand back from the Protestants, and the latter are at this moment in the enjoyment of so many unjust privileges, and in possession of so much plundered from the former, that it will be long before both parties can meet without animosity and jealousy. The great landlords have not yet taken a step towards resigning the least part of their unjust rights over their tenants, and a partition and dissolution of the great estates has not been even dreamt of. In short, a reconciliation is yet so distant, that, in despair, one might almost exclaim, in the words of Moore—

> When will this end, ye Powers of God
> She weeping asks for ever
> But only hears, from out that flood,
> The demon answer,—'Never!'

The religious dissensions and differences of Ireland claim the traveller's attention, especially at Belfast, for here he enters the central point of a new branch, not only of manufactures, but also of religion, namely, the Presbyterian. The three religions of Ireland, the Presbyterian, the Episcopalian, and the Roman Catholic, correspond with the three races which inhabit it, —with the descendants of the original Irish, and of the earliest English colonists, who are all Catholics; with those of the later English immigrants, who are Protestants; and with the Scottish, who profess Presbyterianism. The principal seat of the Episcopalians is undoubtedly Dublin, where they are most powerful by means of the university; but they are scattered every where through the land, as its lords and masters. The stronghold of the Presbyterians is Belfast, where their 'Moderator,' the head of their church, resides, and their general assembly is held. They compose the greater part of the population in the northern districts of Ireland; while in the south the Presbyterians are but few, as in Dublin, *Dungannon*, &c. The Catholics have no such central city, yet there are genuine Catholic towns, as Cork, Galway, Drogheda, &c. They form every where the principal mass of the population. In the north alone, they have been dislodged en masse by the Presbyterians, who have taken their places.

The Presbyterians in Ireland form a separate church of their own, organized on the model of that of Scotland, and called the Presbyterian Church of Ireland, or Ulster, which is its peculiar province. Its foundation dates from the year 1642, and it has therefore existed just 200 years. At different times, as in the Kirk of Scotland, various secessions and reunions have taken place in the bosom of this Irish Presbyterian Church. These schisms were principally caused by the general synods, which had retained the strict orthodoxy of Calvin, Knox, and the Scotch reformers requiring that Presbyterian ministers should subscribe the Confession of Faith framed in the year 1644, by the assembly of the Presbyterian divines at Westminster. This Confession of Faith exactly corresponds with the decisions of the synod of Dortrecht, and contains the most strict Calvinism ever comprised in any creed. When many preachers afterwards objected to signing this Confession, claiming for every one the right of a perfectly free interpretation of the Scriptures, there arose a division of the Presbyterians into Seceders or Nonsubscribers and orthodox Calvinists. At the head of the former stood the Secession Synod; at the head of the latter, the Great Synod of Ulster. In the year 1840 these two synods were again united into a General Assembly. A few congregations only have not assented to this reunion, and now form separate synods of their own. For instance, there is the Presbytery of Antrim, consisting of nine churches, which seceded so early as 1720; then there is the Remonstrant Synod, or, as it is also called, the Reformed Presbyterian Synod of Ireland, which consists of four presbyteries, or twenty-six congregations, who maintain the principle of nonsubscription to creeds. From these twenty-six congregations, five have lately seceded, at the annual assembly in 1840, and again form a little body of their own. The members of the last-named community are principally Unitarians, who worship God the Father solely and alone. The Lord Jesus Christ they consider the Son of God and Ambassador of the Father, the divinely appointed and inspired Saviour of man from the evils of ignorance and sin. But they do not regard him as God, nor do they reverence him as such. They deem the Holy Ghost to be a power, virtue, or agency, which emanates from the Father. On these points all Irish Unitarians agree; but concerning a variety of less important points they hold an equal variety of opinions. These Unitarians have, however, less in common with our German Rationalists than this might lead one to suppose. 'We do not maintain that form of rationalism preached by Paulus, Ammon, and Strauss in your country,' said an esteemed Unitarian minister to me; 'although, indeed, some of us are not unacquainted with the writings of these men.' This is very true: a German Rationalist, and an Irish Unitarian, are two very different beings.

As the subscription of the Westminster Confession of Faith produced the Nonsubscribers, so the circumstance that the various presbyteries did not insist upon perfectly unconditional and unqualified subscription, —that some did not desire any subscription at all, —that others permitted an addition like this: 'We subscribe the Westminster Confession of Faith in so far as it is founded upon holy writ and agreeable to it,'—all this, I say, had the effect of causing many rigorous congregations, who insisted on strict subscription, to unite and form Presbyterian bodies of their own. These are, the Covenanters, who have thirty-five congregations in Ireland; and the Anti-bounty Seceders, who form about nine or ten. All these have no connection with their brother Presbyterians.

On the whole, there are now about four hundred and ninety Presbyterian congregations in Ireland, which are divided into about forty presbyteries. The whole Presbyterian population, in the year 1834, amounted to 642,000 souls; but now it is supposed to far exceed 800,000. The Unitarians have forty congregations, or societies, consisting of 42,000 souls.

The province of Ulster had, in 1831, a population of 2,386,000, and it now probably amounts to 2,500,000: nearly the third part, therefore, is Presbyterian. In Belfast, the proportion of the Presbyterians to other religious communities is computed as follows: —

Presbyterians	23,600
Catholics	19,700
Episcopalians	16,300
Other sects	1,100
Total	60,700

The most remarkable feature in the spirit of the Presbyterian Church is its missionary and proselytizing zeal, which has increased greatly in influence and extent since the reunion of the two great Presbyterian bodies, in 1840. First, there is a foreign mission, for India and other foreign countries; then, since 1841, a Jewish mission, for the conversion of the Jews, which, in conjunction with similar societies in Glasgow and Edinburgh, has sent missionaries to Pesth and Jassy, 'to labour among the seed of Abraham for the everlasting gospel.' And, finally, there is also a home mission, which is the most interesting of all. This home mission has three objects: first, to promote the building of churches in the north of favoured Ulster; second, to reanimate declining congregations, and to establish new ones in the south and west of Ireland; and, thirdly, to instruct, in the knowledge of the Gospel, through the medium of their own tongue, those who speak the Irish language only.

As these subjects are all new, highly interesting, and little known to us, I will here give a short account of the home mission from MacCombe's *Christian Remembrancer* for 1842, and will avail myself of the words of the essay itself, which are very characteristic of the opinions and language of the Presbyterians: —

'Since her purification and renovation, the Presbyterian Church has been ever engaged in the labour of evangelizing Ireland. It is highly edifying that the last exertions of the church, with regard to India and the Jews, have rather strengthened than weakened her home operations. Thirty years ago the missionary system of this church was founded, and every succeeding year has brought it increased activity and resources. But the labours of the last two years have been especially crowned with success, which is chiefly to be attributed to the reunion of the Secession Synod with the Synod of Ulster. There are still, however, some very God-forsaken districts in our favoured Ulster, where the blessings of gospel-preaching cannot be enjoyed by the Protestant population with the desired convenience. Thus many immortal souls remain neglected in the midst of a flood of gospel light. The formation of new congregations, the building of new churches, the appointment of ministers, are the points to which the activity of the mission has been particularly directed, and never has a similar undertaking by any other church been so visibly blessed. In a period of ten years, the number of congregations has been doubled, and some of the strongest and healthiest congregations of Ireland have been produced by this system. The work grows every year in magnitude and importance. No less than fifty-six congregations, in the north of Ireland, now receive pecuniary support from the mission, and but eleven of these are still without a minister. The pressing necessity for the second difficult labour of the mission, again to revive declining congregations, is self-evident. In all the principal towns of the south of Ireland, and even in some country districts, Presbyterian churches once existed and flourished; but during the last fifty years many of them have, from various causes, fallen into decay, and not a few are completely extinct. Moreover, we find, in the south of Ireland, single Presbyterians scattered over the country, and in every town, many of whom are seventy miles and more from a Presbyterian clergyman. The southern division of the home mission has therefore the restoration of the candlestick for the object of its labours.'

'In Cork, Clonmel, Athlone, Galway, Carlow, and other important posts, where very promising congregations now exist, this object has been already effected. We have every reason to believe, that, by the establishment of these congregations in the midst of a benighted land, a vast deal of good has been already done; not only because many precious souls will now be thereby trained and fitted for immortal glory and happiness, but particularly because now a lasting testimony for the truth is deposited even in the midst of surrounding superstition and infidelity. During the last eight months this work has been carried on with particular success by two missionaries, Simpson and Knox, who were sent out to reconnoitre the land. By their exertions very promising openings and congregations have been called to life at Wexford and New Ross. Tralee, (the best centre for the exertions of all missionaries in Ireland,) Killarney, Miltown, Bandon, are points in which the exertions of the church have been crowned with remarkable success. But the work of the dissemination of truth will not be fully carried out, till every Presbyterian, and every Protestant of every creed, has the ordinances of the gospel near at hand. He alone who has himself visited these places, and knows the extent of their abandonment, can fully estimate the importance and the necessity of erecting in the country the standard of the cross.'

'The last, and perhaps the most important, object of the exertions of the home mission, concerns the bestowing the knowledge of the gospel on the Irish-speaking population of our island, almost a third of the entire population. And yet for such a mass of immortal souls not the least sympathy has hitherto been shown, even by the Protestant church. Most of them are totally ignorant of the English language, and no attempt has been made to approach them by another medium. The Presbyterian Church at last has lately resolved to give the gospel to these people in their own language, and for this object it employs two means. The first is, preaching in the Irish tongue. This was long a pious wish in our country. It is now at last in our power to apply this means. During the past year (1841) the Rev. Henry MacManus, who, with great fluency and strength, can address his countrymen in the language they love, has travelled about every where, preaching the word. He has already visited the towns of Galway, Sligo, Clifden, Westport, Drumcornwick, Brickhill, Boyle, and other places in the west. He has also travelled through a great part of the northwest. The reception he almost every where met with was very favourable, and the readiness and the desire of the people to hear him was so great, that one may entertain the hope that the time of grace for our country, even the set time, is at last arrived. The second means is, the erection of Irish schools. There are about three millions of Irish who speak the Irish language, and love it as their mother tongue. In the year 1818, a Bible was printed, in the Irish language and character, by the British and Foreign Bible Society; and the work of circulating the Scriptures among the Irish-speaking population then begun, has now ripened into the present system of teaching and learning through the medium of the Irish language. The schools are very simply contrived, and can be quickly increased to any amount at pleasure. A suitable person is appointed as teacher, in every district where a school is wanted; the pupils are his neighbours and relatives, to the distance of two or three miles round him. They meet alternately at each other's houses for instruction, every evening, after their work is done, and on the Lord's Day, morning and evening. They begin to read and to spell in a little primer, which has been written and printed for them; when they have learned this by heart, a portion of Scripture is put into their hands; they then begin and continue to study the word of God, till they are able to read it with ease and fluency, while at the same time they learn to translate it into English. A portion of it they learn by heart also. The schools are visited thrice a year by an inspector, who reports on their condition to the superintendent. All the teachers very frequently meet at the superintendent's, to be further instructed in the saving doctrines of the Bible, and to be encouraged in the business of teaching, by little premiums and presents. Besides all this, Scripture-readers are engaged to travel about from village to village, and from house to house, in order to maintain among the people the habit of reading and hearing the word of salvation.'

'This entire system of Irish teaching was established by the Presbyterian Church in the beginning of 1835. In the first year, 30 schools were founded; since then they have gone on increasing in number, and in this present 1842 they amount to 223. The scholars last year examined in these schools by the inspectors, amounted to 5407, all Roman Catholics, who learned to read the Holy Scriptures in Irish, and to translate them into English. Not one of these scholars was younger than fifteen, and many hundreds were over fifty and seventy years of age. Many of the teachers have even renounced the errors of Popery, and the knowledge of the Light is making rapid progress among them all. The field of our activity is wide, the necessity great, and the machinery is good. What might not a fully united, zealous, and vigorous Presbyterian Church accomplish, if she called forth all the powers that stand at her command!'

So much for the remarkable activity of the Presbyterian church of Ireland, which calls itself pre-eminently a missionary and an apostolic church.

The Irish Sunday-schools, which differ from those above described, by being open merely on Sunday, and conducted by unpaid teachers, mostly originate from this Presbyterian Church, as the following interesting view of the number of Sunday-schools in the various provinces of Ireland clearly shows. The first society for the formation of Sunday-schools was founded in 1809, and on the 1st of January, 1841, there were, —

Schools	Pupils	Unpaid teachers
In Ulster: 2,010	with 169,377	and 15,891
In Leinster: 455	with 33,540	and 2,969
In Munster: 394	with 19,094	and 2,045
In Connaught: 169	with 8,668	and 763
In all Ireland	3,028	with 230,679 and 21,668

Here again it is apparent how greatly education has been neglected in the west of Ireland, since in Ulster there are single counties in which the Sunday-schools contain from four to five times as many pupils and teachers as the whole five counties of Connaught put together.

The Presbyterians of the north are as unwearied in their exertions in the field of scientific inquiry as in that of religious enlightenment. The whole north of Ireland, 'the favoured Ulster,' in this respect, as far out-shines the rest of Ireland, as Scotland does the rest of Great Britain; and just as the Scotch are superior to the English in education and enlightenment, so are

60

the people of Ulster to the rest of the Irish. Belfast is at once the Edinburgh and Glasgow of Ireland, on a smaller scale. Like Edinburgh, it is the seat of many learned and scientific societies: of horticultural, agricultural, statistical, literary, and historical societies, of a mechanics' institute, a society of natural history, and, lastly, of several musical societies. I visited the institutions and collections of some of these societies.

The society of natural history possesses a little museum, in a handsome and elegant building. This is one of the numerous museums which have of late years been established in all the towns of England; but, upon the whole, the museums of our middle-class German towns are not only older, but richer, and in better order than these British provincial museums. The museum of Belfast contains many interesting Irish antiquities, found in the neighbourhood, and also curiosities of natural history; but here, to his disappointment, the traveller seeks in vain for what, above all things, he has the best right to expect, —I mean a complete, well-arranged, satisfactory, and instructive collection of every thing illustrative of the Giant's Causeway, and, in general, of all the interesting volcanic formations of the north of Ireland. Every provincial museum has no doubt its particular function, since each is generally directed to the investigation of some one important department of natural history. Belfast this great city so rich in scientific materials and learned men, is, without doubt, above all things called upon to exert all its powers to collect in its museum every thing calculated to convey to the inquiring, information and a clear conception of a natural phenomenon, for which the north of Ireland is celebrated throughout the entire world, namely, of those remarkable basaltic formations on its coast.

Some specimens of those coasts are, of course, found in the Belfast museum; but when I think how nobly illustrative many of our German provincial museums are of the geological structure of their neighbourhoods, as the Prague museum of the formation of Bohemia, and the wonderfully arranged collections in Graz illustrative of the structure of the Alps, with regret I must say that in this respect Belfast is far behind them. In vain the traveller inquires after a complete collection of all the volcanic masses of which the northern coast consists, —in vain, for an arrangement of them, according to the order in which nature has disposed them, or for a model of the Giant's Causeway in wood, or for a clear, accurate model in plaster, or any other material, of the entire northern coast, —all of which it is a disgrace to Belfast not to possess. The traveller, *going* to visit this wonder of nature with his head full of expectation, and *returning* from it with his head full of speculations, finds, alas! nothing, or at least very little, of all these things here.

In general the stranger finds more to interest him in the private than in the public collections of the English. The former are usually much richer, and kept in the most admirable order; whilst the latter seem to be only in the course of formation. Of the private collections of pictures, compared to the public, this is very different; and the public libraries, which form the oldest of all classes of collections in England, are of course an exception; but the finest and best collections of natural history and antiquities are generally those of private persons, who zealously devote themselves to some particular branch. In Belfast, there are some private collections unique in their kind, such as Dr. Drummond's wonderful collection of sea plants, and Dr. Thompson's complete and elegantly arranged collection of shells.

The Botanic Garden of Belfast was laid out in 1830, and a great many English botanic gardens have been established within the last twenty years. I was invariably surprised by the extreme youth of all these scientific institutions in England, which has still to accomplish for its remote districts what we have long since done in Germany. The Belfast Botanic Garden is, next to that of Dublin, the finest in Ireland, and as excellent as any in England. It has some advantages over that of Dublin; for although these cities are only eighty miles apart, their climates are very different, the summer at Dublin being much warmer, and the winter more severe, than at Belfast. The enlightened director of the garden, who told me this, thought that this fact might be explained by Dublin having a great plain on its landward side, while Belfast, being on that side surrounded by high hills, receives all its air from the sea. In this garden the cypress was growing in perfect health in the open air, under the 55th degree of latitude, as also the arbutus, which does not grow wild here, as in the south of the island. For this, however, the north is compensated by the yew, which is peculiar to it. A beautiful collection of heaths ornaments the garden; and among them are seen remarkably large ones, which grow in the bogs of Ireland. One division of the garden, called the British Garden, particularly interested me: it contained a collection, as perfect as possible, of all the plants indigenous to the British Isles. There was here a complete collection of grasses, which are of great importance to British gardeners, who take such pride in beautiful grassy lawns. Here I saw no less than 400 species of grass, all indigenous in England. In the larger English towns there are gardens in which grasses only are cultivated, and the production of these, and the sale of their seeds, form a distinct branch of trade. The *festuca ovina*, the *poa trivialis*, the poa *nemoralis*, are grasses which make a good thick, fresh, short verdure, and are therefore much in request for lawns. Australian plants also thrive very well in the temperate atmosphere of Belfast, and in general through all Ireland; and among these are many already diffused far and wide through the Irish gardens. The Irish myrtle was cited to me as an example. This introduction of plants from all parts of the world into England, which has no very rich herbarium of its own, increases daily. A rose, originally brought from China, is now common in Ireland, where it flourishes winter and summer in the open air.

Of musical societies, there are now four in Belfast, —the Anacreontic, the Choral, the Harmonic, and the Society of Harpers, all of which give frequent musical festivals, concerts, and rehearsals. Thalberg, Liszt, and other great musicians, have always visited Belfast, whilst they have neglected Limerick, Cork, and other towns of the south. I mention this, because it is well known that other manufacturing towns, as Manchester and Birmingham, are famous for their musical taste, and their numerous musical societies and festivals; whilst Liverpool, and other trading towns, are as inferior to them in this respect, as Edinburgh is to the manufacturing Glasgow; and because the question may be raised, whether, in manufacturing towns, particular circumstances prevail, which are favourable to the development and cultivation of a taste for music?

The Harpers' Society is the oldest musical society in Ireland. It was founded and supported in a singular manner, at the suggestion of some Irish patriots residing in the East Indies, who were probably more affected by the beautiful Irish melodies, when they sang them among themselves, far from their native land, and who contributed funds for the instruction of some blind boys as harpers at Belfast, and to establish concerts there on this old national instrument. Perhaps a few patriotic Irishmen, in the East Indies or China, will some day, mindful of the wonders of their fatherland, send money to Belfast for the formation of a geological museum, to illustrate the Giant's Causeway, and every thing connected with it.

———

I have already mentioned the Harpers' Society at Drogheda. In the last century there were no such societies in Ireland; and from this one might suppose that harp-playing was now again beginning to flourish, as in the time of the bards of old. But in this we would perhaps deceive ourselves as much, as if from the present schools, professorships, and other exertions for the Irish, Gaelic, and Welsh languages, we were to expect their revival. Sympathies and exertions like these are wont to arise only when an art or science is on the decline; and are often a sign less of its vigour than of its death, like the last flaring-up of an expiring flame. In respect to language, there is no doubt of this. In respect to the harp we cannot decide. Yet Dr. Bunting, who has published a collection of national Irish melodies and a dissertation on Irish music, assures us, that, admirably as some living harpers still play the Irish compositions on the harp, not one of them comes near to those who were present at the great musical meeting at Belfast, in the year 1792, and the most distinguished of whom were, Denis Hempson, Arthur O'Neill, Charles Fanning, and seven others. So much is certain, that the Belfast Harp Society has not fulfilled the expectations it excited, and that it is now dissolved.

Among the other public institutions of Belfast, as in all towns of Ireland, and in all manufacturing towns of England, the fever hospital claims the attention of the traveller. The excessively crowded dwellings of the labouring classes, and the increase of wretchedness and poverty, augment the dangers arising from contagious fever to an extraordinary degree, and render the question of fever hospitals, their better arrangement, and their extension, one of pressing importance to the municipal authorities and the Government of England. As I visited this hospital, and as my friends supplied me with the reports of its operations, I may be able to supply my readers with some interesting information concerning it. From the tables of the number of patients received into the hospital, it appears that, fever has been constantly increasing. From the year 1818 to 1836, the number annually admitted usually amounted to between 300 and 600. The highest number during that period was 1621. In the year 1837, the number amounted to 1987; and in 1838 it rose to the unparalleled one of 3363. Since then, indeed, the number has again diminished, but it has never been less than 1000. The average of six years, previous to 1837, was 750 annually; and of the six years since 1837, upwards of 1500. These numbers are not proportionate either to the increase of the population or the extension of the hospital. In malignity and obstinacy, these Irish fevers appear to be on the increase; for the periods of their prevalence seem to be always growing longer. Before the year 1818, an epidemic infectious fever never lasted in Belfast longer than eight months. In 1818, an epidemic lasted ten months; and in 1836, there was one that continued over a year,—the longest ever heard of here. These fevers prevail almost solely among the poorer classes, and are caused by their bad food and wretched mode of life. Every wet year, which injures the harvest, also produces an increase of fever. When the wealthy are attacked by fever, they are attacked with greater violence and more fatally. Certain localities of this town suffer more from fever than others. This is also the case in Manchester, Glasgow, and other towns, where these epidemics prevail. It is remarkable, that none of all my ten reports showed that season had any influence upon the fever, but that it appeared to prevail with equal severity the whole year round.

To the report for last year is appended a table, showing the occupations of the patients, which gives an idea of what classes suffer most from fever. This table will not be completely available until it is accompanied by a statement of the number of persons in the various trades and callings in Belfast. Among 2056 patients, 704, or more than one-third, were millworkers and weavers. There were but six bleachers, although the number of this class in Belfast undoubtedly bears a far greater proportion to the entire population. 423, or more than a fifth part of these patients, were of the class of servants. It is also remarkable that females appear more liable to fever than males. In almost every year there were in the hospital from ten to twenty per cent, more women than men. Yet the fever is not so violent and fatal to the former as to the latter; for nearly all the tables show that the deaths of the men exceeded those of the women by ten or twenty per cent. The cause of this may be, that the men, on whose labour the subsistence of their families principally depends, are not sent into the hospital until the disease has become very violent. Fever seldomer attacks persons of advanced age, but when it does it is the more violent.

The coast of Antrim

Precautions Before Starting—Stormy Weather—Lough Belfast—The Castle of Carrickfergus—Larne—County of Antrim—Black and White—Limestone and Basalt—The Antrim Coast Road—Boulders—Island Magee—Ballygally Head—Puffing Holes—Knockdhu—Glenarm—The Antrim Family—The McDonnell's and Mac Donnells—The Genealogy of the O'Nialls—Printed and Unprinted Histories of Ireland—Preventive Men—Glenariff—The Old Irish—Caverns—Nanny Murray—Castle Carey—The Antrim Shepherdesses—Fingal and Ossian—Ossian's Grave—Ossian and St. Patrick—Gift of the Gab—'We are Nearly Alone'—Lights—The Maidens—The Heroic Girl—Ballycastle—Lasses!—The Mac Donnells

After I had considered from what side the wind blew, had looked to see whether the coachman had an 'apron' or not, allowed an immoderately stout dame, a rarity in Ireland, to mount the coach, in order to avoid being her neighbour,—in short, after I had made a multitude of inquiries and reflections, which a prudent traveller should not neglect when looking for a seat on the outside of an English stage-coach in bad weather,—after doing all this, I fixed myself in the chosen place to travel to Carrickfergus. A fearful storm was blowing from the north, and rain and hail, lashed by the tempest, alternately poured down on us. It was the first day that I ever heard the Irish allow that the weather was bad. Every where on the road the people added to their good-morrow,—'A wild day to-day!' Inside our coach, we had as ballast only four young ladies, who filled indeed the narrow space allowed for inside passengers in English stage-coaches, but who appeared to be no great ballast to enable us to resist the fury of the storm, which we on the top, who were most exposed to it, dreaded every moment would upset the coach; and therefore, with our heads wrapped up in our cloaks, we huddled close together, in order to afford the less resistance to the force of the wind. The autumn leaves flew like snow in the blast; the trees on the shore bowed like twigs before the storm; the waves dashed against the strand; the sea-gulls screamed, as with difficulty they fluttered landwards; the fish retired to the depths of the ocean; the boats knocked against the shore: in short, it was just such uproarious weather as one should desire when he intends to visit the famous Giant's Causeway, and the whole of the volcanic, Vulcan-forged coast of the north-eastern extremity of Ireland. A storm occasions many interesting spectacles on this coast, as we will soon perceive, and harmonizes better than fair weather with the wild work of the giants. When these mountains arose from the abysses of the earth—when these rocks fell shattered and hissing into the sea, or dashed together on the land—when the giants paved their causeway, and the Cyclops bored holes, and hollowed out caverns, and formed rock-bridges, and rugged precipices, and gaps, and bold headlands here—was the weather then calm and sunny!

The road runs first along the shore of Lough Belfast. The Irish sometimes call even those waters loughs which are not completely surrounded by land, but have an out-let into the sea; particularly those which, like Lough Foyle, have but a narrow opening, and which we would call Haffs. Lough Belfast is, however, an instance of a lough with an extraordinarily large opening. As the southern coast of Ireland has its so-called harbours, the western its bays, the eastern neither bays nor harbours, at least very few—so has the northern its loughs, such as Lough Belfast, Lough Strangford, Lough Larne, Lough Foyle, &c. Lough Belfast is also called Lough Carrickfergus, after the town of the same name, which, as that name shows, is one of the oldest in Ireland. Long before an Englishman set foot on Ireland's soil, and before the Scotch had yet laid a stone of Belfast, Carrickfergus was a place of note. In Ireland there are many examples of the old Irish towns being abandoned and allowed to go to ruin by the English and Scotch, and of new ones being built in their neighbourhood.

On the whole way from Belfast to Carrickfergus garden follows garden, and country seat follows country seat; but to these tiny productions of man the storm and the surf did not add beauty, as they did to those vast works of the giants to which we were hastening; and as the hail obliged us to keep our eyes closed, all the capital spun out of flax, and laid out in flowers, shrubberies, cottages, and parks, did not bring us the least tribute of enjoyment.

Near Carrickfergus, a large old castle runs out into the sea: it is fortified even now, and is garrisoned by two companies of soldiers. Its situation is very picturesque, and the views of the opposite coast, the town of Bangor, the lough, and the wide sea, must be charming, when Boreas does not interpose a screen between the eye and the prospect. The walls of the castle are at the same time surrounded by the green ivy, and the white foam of the waves that break against its base. At this castle William III. landed, before he fought the battle of the Boyne. Here the French attempted to land, in order to help the Irish when it was too late. Here, or at some other point in the neighbourhood, was the chief landing-place of the entire north of Ireland; and every expedition, whether friendly or hostile, from Great Britain, particularly from the north of Scotland, disembarked here. The entire coast, further towards the north, is bound by rugged rocks and threatening cliffs. Lough Belfast was here for Scotland, what Bantry Bay, in the south-west, was for Spain and the Phoenicians; what Waterford and Wexford was for the English.

The Belfast stage-coach goes no farther than Carrickfergus. From thence to the next little village, Larne, a two-horse car conveys the traveller, who, on his arrival there must himself provide his own conveyance, or join her Majesty's letter-bag, which is carried northwards by a one-horsed car. The little Lough Larne, which is sheltered on every side by hills, and has but a very narrow mouth, was studded with small barks, probably fishing boats, which had come in here for shelter. Flocks of sea-birds, which also seemed to dread sea-sickness, were fluttering around the boats.

Larne is a quiet little town, like many in the north of Ireland. From Larne the coast begins to assume its picturesque and wild volcanic character, and here I joined the aforesaid leather letterbag. 'Her Majesty's Mail' is here a little low two-wheeled car, of the kind I have already described. The passenger sits on one side, the driver on the other. The horse gets forward as well as he can, and the equipage follows after him. I could not help contrasting this with the majestic four-horsed mails in England.

All the land lying between the sea, Lough Neagh, Lough Belfast, and the river Bann, is called the county of Antrim. This entire tract, so rich in wonders, is covered with a great stratum of limestone. Over this limestone, volcanic masses, probably thrown up from beneath, have been deposited, and have disturbed the arrangement and composition of the original stratum, which in some places is even entirely removed, and in others depressed, or at least covered or shattered in pieces, and thrown aside. This limestone, or hard chalk, is snow-white wherever it is disclosed to the eye; the volcanic masses are chiefly basalt, and, where it is uncovered, is dark-coloured and black. The circumference of this district of limestone and basalt is about one hundred and twenty miles; and the stretch of coast in which the mixture of these formations is apparent, from Lough Belfast to Lough Foyle, is about sixty miles in length. Along this entire stretch of coast, the white chalk-rocks appear mixed up with the black volcanic formations in the most manifold combinations, and compose most interesting and picturesque forms.

Sometimes the chalk-mass is deposited in level strata, and over it is formed the basalt in strata equally regular. In many places, the limestone has remained quite untouched by the basalt, and its white cliffs project defyingly into the sea, as they once stood amid the glowing volcanic liquids. In other places they disappear beneath the surface of the sea, as if the basalt had pressed them down. This basalt appears partly in columns, and partly in shapeless masses. It often forms long rows of thick high columns, arranged like organ pipes, or groves of trees, along the coast; it frequently yawns into caverns, stops short in rugged points, springs into the sea with bold overhanging cliffs, or breaks up into little dismembered rocks and pointed islands. In other places, again, the limestone and the basalt seem to have struggled violently with one another for the mastery, while their colours and materials alternate in short patches.

The effects of all these operations and occurrences are, of course, only visible on the coast, and at those spots where the rocks are not covered with earth and vegetation, as they mostly are. Here and there the land rises into some lofty points, which, however, do not exceed 2000 feet; and here and there the masses sink, forming valleys which open out on the sea. Along the sides of these valleys, the basalt and limestone rocks stand in rugged rows, as if they were caused by great convulsions and yawnings of the earth. The good cultivation of these valleys, the black basalt rocks along their sides, the waterfalls which dash down from the precipices, the wide sea at their entrances,—all this must make some of them delightful places of residence. The coast itself, except at the mouths of these valleys, is lined with rugged cliffs. Many headlands and summits rise to a height of from 1000 to 1200 feet, but their usual height is from 600 to 1000.

The nearest of these valleys, after passing Larne, is Glenarm, and then the valleys of Glenariff and Cushendun. A narrow and steep way, called 'the Path,' formerly led the traveller along this coast. Very lately, a beautiful road, called the 'Antrim Coast Road,' has been substituted for this path, which worked its way, as well as it could unaided by art, over the basaltic and limestone rocks. After the description I have given of this coast, it may be concluded that the formation of a perfectly level road was here an undertaking of no ordinary difficulty. When one sees the work itself, he must in fact confess that neither powder nor pickaxe was spared, and that no great tenderness was shown to the rocks. On the contrary, the English have here cut an arrow-straight road, in spite of Vulcan and basalt, and have transmitted to coming ages a work for which posterity will long be thankful. Here and there vast masses of rock have been cut through, from their summit to their base; in other places, gaps and chasms have been filled up, and the road runs as if on a wall. These parts of the road, where vast masses of limestone were wont to roll down from the slippery steeps, presented peculiar difficulties. The English call these loose blocks of stone 'Boulders,' or 'Boulder-stones.' Many of them still break away from the walls of rock, being gradually loosened by the effects of time and weather. Others, long since shattered, lie strewn about on the rocks, or on the clay which here and there covers the rock, and then, after a long continuance of wet weather, they tumble down, bringing the clay along with them. At such places it was therefore necessary to protect the road with a kind of half-arch, so that the boulder stones might roll harmlessly over it; or to build a solid wall, of immense pieces of rock, to prevent the stones from falling into the road. The boulder-stones which have rolled down ages ago, form here and there a dam against the assaults of the sea.

Such, then, was the coast and the coast road along which our letter-bag, and those who accompanied it, rolled away through the storm. Near Larne, the long, little peninsula, called Island Magee, which bends around Lough Larne, nearly touches the coast with its point. This peninsula is also of volcanic formation,—a dam built of columns of basalt. Along its entire eastern coast, column-like basalt cliffs are ranged, for the length of four or five miles, and are known by the name of The Gobbins. This basaltic peninsula, which is from a mile to a mile and a half wide, and six or seven miles long, is the true Giant's Causeway of this coast: the so-called Giant's Causeway is mere child's play compared to it. But as the peninsula is covered with vegetation on the upper surface, the pavement of columnar basalt is not visible, and the smaller work has therefore borne off the greater name.

The next interesting point is Ballygally Head, which projects majestically and boldly into the sea, and is formed of a countless number of vast, rudely-formed basalt columns. After the Gobbins, it is the second place where the columns are exposed to the light of day. The road leads round the principal mass of the headland, and the most extreme and somewhat lower point is alone cut off. As the greater portion of the road runs along the edge of the water, the most interesting sights were every where presented by the fury of the storm, that seemed to turn up the very depths of the sea. The mighty waves broke wildly against the great boulder-stones, of all sizes, which lay scattered on the shore. Roaring they came smoothly along, like moving mountains, till all at once they tumbled on the boulder-stones, and were shattered and dashed to pieces like shipwrecked vessels. The majestic crystal-green water-mountains bounded against the rocks, and, with a hollow crash, broke into hundreds of big and little streams, which quickly and busily lost themselves between the boulders. Twenty white foaming fountains shot up at once, and single arms of the great wave tumbled over the rocks, forming momentary cascades, which, though mere improvisations, for an instant presented a more beautiful spectacle than many a far-famed waterfall in the county of Wicklow. Thousands and thousands of waves thus marched in fierce assault against the shore, and burst, one after the other, like the rockets of an artfully-contrived firework, into most picturesque and curious forms.

As we approached the entrance of the valley of Glenarm, I remarked a strange column of smoke, that seemed to rise from the topmost edge of the rocks. As I could neither suppose a dwelling nor so great a turf-fire here, I asked the driver what this smoke came from. 'It is not smoke, your honour,' he replied, 'but the water of a waterfall, which is carried up into the air by the storm.' At first I could not bring myself to believe this; but I afterwards convinced myself that the phenomenon of a waterfall being carried up into the air by a strong north wind, was not unusual on this coast. At one place I saw, on the highest edge of the cliff, three similar columns of water-dust in a row together. They were driven to and fro by the wind: now they rose higher, now lower; but never ceased for an instant, like fountains driven by some constantly working machinery. The edge of the rocks is here and there very steep, and at the same time full of narrow clefts in the basalt. In these clefts, the waterfalls, in calm weather, pursue their picturesque course in quite a natural manner; but when the north wind rages against the lofty cliffs, it rushes up with peculiar violence through the crevices, as through pipes in which the currents of air are compressed, and carries up with it the water it meets, like dust into the air.

I afterwards discovered similar fountains of water-dust on the low coasts. These are almost still more remarkable. Next day, I saw them near the

Giant's Causeway, a few hundred paces from the road. As I was driving over a low grassy headland, and did not perceive that the sea was behind it, they looked like fountains rising from the ground, in the midst of meadows. They swayed to and fro in the wind like the others, and rising to a height of forty or fifty feet, scattered a shower far and wide around them on the meadow. Approaching nearer, I found that they proceeded from the sea. Here too, on the low coast, were sharp little clefts and indentations in the basaltic pavement, into which the wind drove the water, and catching it in little whirlwinds, carried it up in fountains of spray. In some places, these fountains sprang up with peculiar force, only with every rising wave. At others, where the coast was so formed that the wind was driven upwards in a continuous current, carrying the water with it from the surface, the fountains were quite constant. On other parts of the Irish coast, of similar formation, these fountains are also to be seen; as, for instance, on the coast of the county of Clare, where the Irish call them salt-water fountains, and the holes from which they spring, 'puffing-holes.'

The white chalky rocks of the coast are full of flint-stones, which are not scattered irregularly through them, but sprinkled or deposited in long horizontal strata, of two or three feet in thickness. These flints often run in long stripes through the white rocks. The inhabitants of the neighbourhood dig them out, and make them an article of trade. Near Glenarm, I saw whole walls of flint-stones, great and small, waiting to be shipped. Not only do these flint-sprinkled chalk-rocks break up into boulder stones, but also the black basalt masses that lie above them. Thus the recesses of the coast, and the little valleys, are all full of black and white blocks of stone, like Jacob's black and white herds. These black and white stones are here mingled every where. The road is mended with them; and all the walls of the gardens, houses, and farm-yards are also built of both kinds mixed.

After passing Ballygally Head, we came to other steep, rugged cliffs and masses of rock, called the Sallagh-braes, where the white chalk foundation, and the black basalt cap upon it, are plainly seen. A great mass of basalt has been severed from the rest, and lies, like a floundering whale, in the midst of the breakers, near the coast. The Irish call it Knockdhu, or the black rock. Further out in the sea, about four miles from the shore, lie some other rocks, called The Maidens, on two of which lighthouses have been erected. Still further off, one of the south-western headlands of Scotland is seen raising its head above the waves. It is the Mull of Cantire, with the little isle of Sanda.

The most beautiful point of the coast is Glenarm, which, on account of the many charms assembled here, is one of the most delightful spots in Ireland. The castle, which is the residence of the Antrim family, as well as the little town near it, and the wide valley behind it, bears the martial name of Glenarm, or the Vale of Arms. Perhaps it has often been the theatre of deeds of arms, as the Scottish heroes used to come over here to light with those of Erin. The valley, too, looks warlike enough. Like two long lines of mail-clad heroes, stand the dusky basalt rocks, leaving a broad and level battle-field between them. They run inland, pretty parallel to each other; and one might suppose that, instead of the present little brook, a large and rapid river once ran down here to the sea. From the black rocks, little waterfalls tumble down, here and there, into the valley, and its moist bottoms are covered with the most lovely green carpet, and partly with groups of stately old trees. In the vicinity of the little town and the castle, all trace of wildness disappears, and every thing assumes the look and order of a delightful park and pretty flower-gardens. The castle itself, to whose benevolent mistress I had an opportunity of paying a visit, is tastefully built in the old Gothic style, and elegantly fitted up,—'a noble mansion, with an air of baronial protection.' Four hundred deer and stags graze around it, and six hundred trees spread their cooling shade over its grounds; and these charming and peaceful scenes, in the very midst of the warlike basalt walls of the well-watered valley, with the waves of the ocean breaking at its very entrance, make this appear as wonderful a situation for a residence as any in the whole world beside.

The period at which the Antrim family came over is no longer accurately known; but their present extensive possessions, and the title of Earls of Antrim, were granted them in 1630 by Charles I. Their family name is McDonnell. To his 'beloved cousin, Randall McDonnell,' Charles I., on the 8th of September, 1630, granted the entire north-western part of the county of Antrim, called the Route, or Root, together with that called the Glyns, the entire island of Rathlin, and the piece of ground called 'the Crags,' as well as the Castle of Dunluce, to be held by knight's service, and to yield for it, on the day of the birth of St. John the Baptist, a cast[1] of good falcons to the Viceroy of Ireland. Old feudal customs like these are in full force in England a the present day: thus the Duke of Wellington is obliged to make a yearly feudal present to the Queen for his lands, which he would lose if he neglected to do so.

The family of McDonnell is spread all over the county of Antrim, and I everywhere met persons of the name, who claimed kindred with the Antrim family. At the other side of the water, in the near part of Scotland, the McDonnells are equally numerous. The Scottish Mac Donnells, and the Irish McDonnells, each claim the greater antiquity for their own family. The former assert that the Irish McDonnells are a younger branch of their clan; and the latter maintain that the Scottish clan is descended from the Irish. This is now merely an ink-shedding genealogical dispute, while in by-gone days it was probably one of a blood-shedding and warlike nature. Some old antiquarians, and possessors of manuscripts, are for ever starting up among both families, and lashing their adversaries with the arms of criticism and satire, to be themselves treated in the same way. Even Walter Scott has joined in the fray, and decided in favour of the higher antiquity of the Irish McDonnells; so, at least, I heard it said on the south-western side of the Channel which runs between the coast of Antrim and the Mull of Cantire.

How high these old Irish and Scotch families carry their genealogical pretensions I had, here in the county of Antrim, an opportunity of again convincing myself; for here I was allowed to inspect the genealogical tree of the celebrated family of the O'Nialls. The O'Nialls are a princely family, were kings of Ulster, and also frequently 'Monarchs of Ireland,' and scions of the most noble house of Heremon. At the top of their genealogical tree stands Adam! This is tolerably modest and unpretending; for, as I have said, many Irish and Scotch families go farther back than Adam: besides, Adam is a very ignoble progenitor, since all vulgar, as well as noble blood, has proceeded from him. After him came many other Bible names. Then came 'Feninsa, King of Scythia, founder of the universal schools of the Plain Magh Scanair,' and 'Heber Glemsiony, Lord of Gothia.' Then followed many insignificant names, down to Dea, who carried a colony from Scythia

---

[1] 'A cast of falcons:' as many at may be cast at once from the hand into the air, [original footnote].

to Galicia in Spain, 1400 years before Christ. After Dea came Bratha, Breogan, Bilius, and Milesius, mere Spanish kings; and at last Heremon, first monarch of Erin. The length of the reigns of most of the kings was also given. Feidtroth, in the third year of whose reign the Saviour was born, came next; and from him the O'Nialls, who still reside in the neighbourhood of Lough Neagh, in the north of Ireland, as lords and earls, trace their descent. This genealogy was in manuscript, like most other copies which are to be found in the bands of those who claim kindred with the head of the clan. They are very seldom printed. The histories of Ireland, given to the light of day by the press, though they are fanciful enough, do not venture on such high flights. Even those Irish who write histories of their fatherland for publication find it often very difficult to relinquish their belief in those manuscripts, and to reject them altogether as unfounded inventions; whilst those who write and read, but do not print, cling with body and soul to those manuscript histories. The next day I continued my journey, again joining her Majesty's one-horsed 'letter-bag.' It was another 'wild day,' for the north wind still blew with equal fury, and our road ran along the coast, as on the day before. To-day we passed Garron Point, and entered the valley of Glenariff. The views on this extent of coast were almost still more beautiful and grand than those we had already seen. Garron Point is a rugged, high point of land, lying there like a footstool before a throne: the road leads over the ridge of land, between the point and the still higher cliffs of the coast. On the projecting summit of the rock lives an English revenue officer, with his people; for all this coast in particular is strongly furnished with coast-guards, because an extensive contraband trade was carried on here by little smuggling vessels, which can easily get between the rocks, and, on account of the wildness of the country, readily transport their goods into the interior. These coast-guards are a kind of amphibia—a kind of middle class between soldiers and sailors; for though their dress is like that of sailors, yet it has also something military in it. Their duty is, from their high station on the rock, to observe every vessel on the sea, to understand how to form a right judgment of them, to guess their destination and designs from their movements and outward appearances; and to oppose the smugglers, as well on land by military operations, as on sea by seamanship.

The valley of Glenariff, which means the Valley of the Caves, is still wider than that of Glenarm. Many other little valleys lie in the neighbourhood, such as Cushendall and Cushendun, and all these taken together bear, in Ireland, the name of 'the Glens,' or 'the Glynns.' These glens, even at the present day, form in, many respects a separate little province in themselves. They lie close together, and being surrounded by high mountains on both sides, have still preserved the old Irish race and language, while to the right and left both have been completely lost by the influence of English and Scotch settlers. 'In the Glens, the people still speak Irish,' I was every where assured; and even the people whom I met on the road understood Irish as well as English,—a circumstance I did not expect here. On the entire east coast of Ireland, those glens, and the country round Drogheda, are, as far as my experience went, the principal and almost the only points where the Irish language still exists. In those glens also, one of the last wolves, some say the last,—in opposition to the Kerry people, whose opinion we have already given,—is affirmed to have been shot in the year 1712.

On the road to Glenariff, and in the valley itself, the mountains and cliffs are partially adorned with a beautiful and natural wood: here are seen hollies, hazels, and whitethorns of great size; while in the valley, are oaks and ash trees. All along the coast numerous caverns and under-ground passages are to be found. Thus, at Garron Point, is a cave, that opens near the surf of the sea, and from which a considerable quantity of water gushes, even, it is alleged, in the driest season. The road passes over the entrance of this cavern. More of these little caverns are seen at the other side of Glenariff, close together, and are called the Caves of Red Bay. The road also passes near their entrances. In one of them a smith had erected his forge, and we found there some remains of his instruments; but it does not appear that this cave is now used. The other cave was still inhabited by Nanny Murray, a maiden well stricken in years, who, as the people informed me, had lived here forty or sixty years, in a word, from time immemorial. I visited this old woman, as all passing pilgrims are wont to do; and one of her friends, who was with her on a visit, kindled a splinter at the fire, by which the old woman sat spinning, and lighted me round to all corners of the cave. The entrance was closed with a low wall, through which a door led; behind was another low division of the cave, in which her bed stood. It was well for me that I had seen all this, for I was afterwards every where asked by every one whether I had been to visit Nanny Murray in the Red-bay Cave. Nanny, as long as I was with her, continued to spin and smoke quite calmly; but when I was about to depart she offered me a dram, and muttered some unintelligible words. I doubted not that I had before me one of those romantic beings who play so conspicuous a part in some of Sir Walter Scott's novels. The cave itself is known far and wide as 'Nanny's Cave.'

Those caves are found in a conglomerate of clay and an immense multitude of flints, exactly like the conglomerate met with at the foot of the Erzgebirge in Saxony, and that is also visible at the Tharander Grund, near Dresden. On the far-projecting summit of this conglomerate mass lies Castle Carey. The way here passes under the rock, which was cut through by the road-makers, and forms an arch over the road. Beyond the arch, under the ruins of the castle, is seen the broad, handsome, arched opening of another cave, from which some sheep, which had there sought shelter from the violence of the storm, were looking out. This entrance, which is in a perfectly perpendicular cliff, is quite inaccessible; but it has another connection with the external world by a long passage which goes through the rock. The sheep walk through this long passage, and then rest in the wide convenient cave, over the precipice. In winter, too, they are penned in there by the shepherds. All the basalt mountains of Antrim are exclusively used for the pasturage of sheep; whilst the neighbouring county of Down is famed throughout Ireland for horses. The latter require the attendance and care of men; but all that is required by the sheep is easily performed by girls; and, in fact, the shepherdesses of Antrim are as much celebrated as their sheep. A verse therefore has been made in allusion to these circumstances, which contains a rhyme very characteristic of Irish pronunciation:

The county of Down for men and horses,
The county of Antrim for lambs and lasses.

As in Nanny Murray I beheld, alive and bodily before me, just such a
personage as one finds depicted in Sir Walter Scott's novels, so in the
valleys of the district of the Glynns I saw such rugged, rocky vales, as are
represented by those painters and engravers, who endeavour to restore to
us, with pencil and graver, the spirit-like forms of Ossian's poetry. Those
Glynns are said to be, even now, full of songs and traditions, which glorify
the deeds of Fingal and Ossian. At Cushendall, there was shown, until
lately, the grave of Dallas, a Scottish hero, who is said to have been slain
here by the hand of Ossian; and the people assured me that those Glynns,
and the entire coast of Antrim, was the true and principal theatre of the
deeds of both those heroes.

Even the Giant's Causeway itself is connected with Fingal; for he,
according to the popular tradition, was the giant who built this road for
himself. The Irish historians inform us that Fingal, as Macpherson, and,
after him, all the rest of Europe, calls him—or Finn-Mac-Cumhal, as the
historians call him, —or Finn-Mac-Cul, as the name is pronounced in
Ireland, —was the son-in-law of the Irish king Cormac, who reigned in the
middle of the third century after Christ, and was the introducer of the
famous Fianna Eirinn (the ancient national guards of Erin). He filled all the
north of Ireland and the west of Scotland with the fame of his exploits; left
to his successors, Ossian and Oscar, the gifts of song and heroism; and fell
by the lance of an assassin in the year 273. Even to this day those parts of
Scotland and Ireland abound with traditions respecting Ossian and Fin-
Mac-Cul, and many natural phenomena are ascribed to those heroes and
called by their names. Thus there is, in the north of Ireland, an Ossian's
Mountain (Mount Alt-Ossoin,) and a great number of caves, lakes, and
mountains, the names of which are compounded with Finn. In the county
of Meath is shown a 'Finn's Rock,' under the shade of which Fingal once
rested, after the chase, with his trusty wolf-hound Brann; also on
Shanthamon mountain are his five fingers, in the shape of five great stones
each five feet high and four tons in weight. There is also a 'Lough na Fenie,'
and a 'Fenian Valley.' Some of the Irish consider the name of Finn as
connected with the Phoenicians, and say that the Phoenicians were the
ancient giants, who cultivated this land, and supplied it with the wonders of
nature, and that Fin-Mac-Cul introduced those Phoenicians into Ireland. In

Scotland, too, there are many valleys, rivers, and mountains named after Fingal, such as Fingal's Cave, in the island of Staffa. The people here appear to have treated Fingal as the Greeks treated Hercules, and, departing from history, to have raised him to a Titan, a god, a great power of nature. We remember the pillars of Hercules, and other wonders of nature ascribed to that hero. Fingal is, in fact, the Hercules of Erin and Caledonia, and of the archipelago of islands lying between them. Nay, the people go so far as to place the grave of Ossian himself in this country, it is said to be in an ancient churchyard of the little neighbouring village of Layde. The ruined church of this grave-yard stands, covered with ivy, on a little eminence near the coast. Other accounts, again, place the bard's grave on the highest peak of the neighbouring mountain, Lurgethan, where there is a cairn, beneath which Ossian is said to repose. The latter account is certainly the most probable: for Ossian, the epic poet, the great hero, would prefer to lie on the peak of a far-seen mountain, from whence he could look far out into the sea, and over all his valleys, rather than down in the back-ground of a bay. Besides, he was a heathen, and in nowise connected with the Christian church. The Irish say, however, that Ossian had a conversation with St. Patrick, and was converted by him to Christianity, though the ancient heathen hero and poet lived 200 years before the saint. There is, indeed, an Irish legend, that Ossian lay sunk in a magic sleep, for 200 years, on the bank of the Shannon, and afterwards had that conversation with St. Patrick, by whom he was awakened. Probably some pious Irishman could not determine to revere Ossian as unbaptized, or permit him to die a heathen. I was told that there is a long and interesting poem, in which this entire story is beautifully related, and the conversation between Ossian and St. Patrick set out at full length. The story is doubtless well worthy of notice, and may be interpreted to mean, that Christianity, although looking on itself as the only true and saving religion, yet in this manner reconciled itself to the good men who were to be found among the heathen, and, in the blessing given to Ossian, in a certain degree included all heathendom retrospectively in the Christian community. Thus understood, it appears to me that this, story of the meeting of St. Patrick and Ossian reflects great honour upon the Irish; and I would like to know if there are similar legends in other Christian lands, by which the people have acknowledged that they wish to be more closely connected with their heathen forefathers by such a reconciliation.

At nightfall we arrived at Cushendall, where we found a woman by a turf fire, who possessed in a high degree the 'gift of the gab,'—plainly one of those gifts which, when the different qualities of mind fell down from heaven on the British islands, flew to the west side of St. George's Channel—none of it fell on the east. To the turf fire, which she blew for me, and at which I warmed my frozen feet—to the glass of whisky which she handed me, and which tasted of turf, like every thing else in Ireland— and to the oat-cake which she gave me with it, she added such a commentary of clack as I never before heard on matters so insignificant. Excellent as had been the entertainment provided for our minds on this journey along the coast, that for our bodies was proportionally bad; for, except one glass of whisky, one little bit of oat-cake, and a couple of gleaming sods of turf, no comfort fell to my lot on this journey. Add to this, the open car, the rain, the storm, and the clack of the woman with the 'gift of the gab,' and it will be readily imagined that it sometimes required all the beauty of the coast of Antrim to compensate for these unpleasant drawbacks. The driver had this advantage, that he had only to travel one stage, and then found another to take his place. As I could not bring myself to stop, I travelled on, exposed to the weather. 'Indeed it is wonderful, sir, that you travel in such a night,' said she with the 'gift of the gab,' as I was again making myself comfortable on the new car, with the aid of some fresh straw, while she lighted me with the lantern, and wished to give me another glass of whisky before starting, which I could not bring myself to touch on account of the repulsive taste of turf. However, people generally say that this turfy taste, which is at first so repulsive to the stranger, is particularly pleasing when one has once become accustomed to it; and I know many national dishes which have a flavour extremely disagreeable to those unaccustomed to them, but with which they afterwards become completely enamoured. Thus there may be also national weaknesses and failings, which people in time take for virtues.

'We are nearly alone, your honour!' remarked my new driver, as we turned landwards into the dark valley beyond Cushendall; for at Cushendall the road to the Giant's Causeway quits the coast, leaving to the right the north-eastern mountains and headlands of Antrim. 'Indeed, Paddy,' I replied, 'I think we are quite alone: perhaps you see some forms of Fingal's heroes, or other beings, in the valley, and on that account you are afraid to say, without reservation, that we are quite alone. Are you afraid lest, if you should say we two are quite alone, some one should speak out from the darkness, 'Ha! Stop! Am not I too here?"' 'Indeed, your honour! don't joke in this way by night. No, indeed, I repeat it, we are almost entirely by ourselves!' 'The storm is here too, Paddy, and we can almost do without your horse (which you seem to have entirely overlooked), and sail over the hills before the wind!'

The night was pitch dark, and if the heroes of Ossian were but as luminous as decaying wood, we must now have seen them the more plainly, as the rain and hail had ceased, and only a dry storm swept over the rocks. When we came up from the valley on to the hills, our prospect became pretty extensive, and we recognised in the darkness five gleaming lights. One shone from a lighthouse on the opposite coast of Scotland, two from lighthouses near the entrance of Lough Foyle, and two others behind us, from 'The Maidens' before described. The two last-mentioned pairs were twenty or twenty-three miles distant, and yet we saw them shimmering through the darkness as plain as stars, which were entirely wanting in our heaven. With what joy must not sailors, returning from America, behold these lights, and what a pleasing feeling of security must they not produce in them whilst engaged in their perilous voyages. 'Particularly, your honour,' Paddy put in his word, 'if they could persuade themselves that in each of those towers there lived such a brave maiden as now lies buried some weeks on the Maiden Rocks. Has your honour heard of this brave girl of the Maiden Rocks, who rescued a great part of a ship's crew?'

I had, in fact, not heard it, although the story was well known through the medium of the newspapers. 'Then you must listen to me, for it is a true story. Near those two lights which stand on two rocks, there are some other reefs, at the distance of about half a mile. A few years ago a ship ran on those reefs in a dark foggy night, when they could not see a cable's length from them. As the weather was uncommonly stormy, both ship and crew were soon reduced to a very deplorable condition, and in this state they were perceived next morning from one of the lighthouses, in which an old man and his daughter performed the duty. The poor sailors shouted for help, and made signals for assistance. But the old man shuddered at the idea of rowing through those raging waves, in a frail boat, to the opposite rocks, and he hesitated to embark in the dangerous attempt. His young daughter, however, a girl not quite twenty years old, moved by the cry of distress from the unfortunates, sprang into the boat, boldly seized the oar, and having persuaded her father to follow her, they both rowed to the wreck, where they took in as many as remained still alive, and, with God's help, brought them safe back to the lighthouse. The girl received the thanks of the rescued and the applause of all Ireland, which filled every newspaper and every mouth with her praises. Large presents were sent to her and her father; advantageous offers of service were also made her, which she rejected, because she wished to remain with her father and her lighthouse. The whole circumstance is celebrated in a play, which has been often acted in London and Dublin. A couple of months ago this heroic girl became sick, and died soon after, and all the papers in Ireland noticed her death with grief. I wonder that some lord, excited by the girl's fame, did not travel to her rock, and woo her. Perhaps this would have happened, had she lived longer; perhaps she would not have died so soon, had a lover taken her from her rock.'

At nine o'clock in the evening we arrived, on the wings of the wind, at Ballycastle. This little port lies near the sea, exactly opposite the well-known island of Rathlin. Here ends the mountainous district of the Glens or Glynns, and now begins a waving, high plain, which terminates towards the sea, in a rugged shore, more or less steep.

With the district of the Glynns ends also the Irish language. The people pointed out to me the little stream which flows eastwards from Ballycastle, as the boundary dividing the English and Irish languages. 'On this side of the bridge,' said they, 'almost all the people speak Irish, but most of them understand English too. But on that side, from Ballycastle westward, no one understands Irish.' For the last couple of miles from Ballycastle, I had a policeman sitting with me on our little car. I asked him if he had much to do here in the Glens. 'Yes,' said he, 'we have much more to do than our companions near Londonderry. The people here in the Glens are more quarrelsome and unquiet than these in Derry, and we must keep careful watch. They would be very mischievous, if they were not so much afraid of the law. In the Glens, too, they are poorer than in Derry; as you must know, since you have travelled so much, that the Catholics are all over the world poorer than the Protestants.' I give this man's testimony in his own words, for I believe there is some truth in it, but I do not venture to say how much.

At last a friendly little inn at Ballycastle opened to us its hospitable doors and calm chambers. We found a right comfortable room, a cheerful tea-table, a homely, warm fire, and by the fire—oh! wonderful! the last part of the before-mentioned popular rhyme about the counties of Down and Antrim: 'The county of Antrim for lambs and lasses!'—lasses, young lasses! They had come, as the hostess told me, to pay a visit to their relative, the Rector of Rathlin; but the violence of the storm had detained them three days on the mainland, there being no fewer than eight fishing boats from Rathlin laid up in the harbour of Ballycastle for still a longer time, not venturing to return home on account of the high sea that ran between the island and the mainland, although the distance was hardly six miles.

I blessed the storm, however, which brought with it consequences so agreeable to me. One must travel in extraordinary weather to meet with extraordinary things; and the traveller in England may indeed call it extraordinary luck if he can take his tea at an inn in the agreeable society of young ladies; for in this country it is the general rule that every one, while sipping this beverage, should shut himself up in his own chamber, and, without troubling himself about his fellow-travellers, enjoy himself alone, or, at the most, whisper in a low tone with his own friends. But in the little inn at this end of the world, there were, besides the common sitting-room, only two small bedrooms; and as the storm and the darkness forbade all escape to Rathlin, necessity thus broke through the barrier even of strait-laced English manners, or rather unmanners. The young ladies were obliged to receive the wet, frozen, very pitiable-looking traveller, and make room for him at the fire, without asking leave of papa and mamma. I cannot deny that a certain love of mischief mingled with my feelings; for when I thought of those little Antrim mice, caught here *nolens volens*[1], I determined to take full revenge on English customs, which condemn the traveller to so many privations and tedious lonesome hours, and not to let them off so entirely undisturbed; that is to say, I resolved to pass the evening pleasantly, conversing with them to my heart's content.

The ladies were, of course, called Misses Mac Donnell; for in this part of the world every respectable person bears that name. My last postilion was called McDonnell, and an honest fellow he was; and even the innkeeper

---

[1] willing or not, [Clachan ed.].

said his name was Mac Donnell. The estate of the young ladies' relation, the island of Rathlin, formed the principal theme of our conversation. Seeing plainly that I must relinquish all hopes of a visit to this island, which I had so much desired, for all told me that no one could take me across in this weather, I was obliged to be content with surveying it in the image which these Antrim lasses set before me; to which I afterwards added as much information as I could myself acquire from the coast next morning, through my telescope.

The Island of Rathlin

Names of the Island—Its Volcanic Origin—Peculiar Tides—Interruption of Communication between Rathlin and Ireland—Robert Bruce—His Successor—Mr. Gage—The Possessors of The Soil—Population of Rathlin—Ponies and Foxes—Preparation of Kelp—The Ushet Men and the Kenramer Men—Grave Mounds—The Campbells—The Monastery of St. Columba

The island of Rathlin, or Rachlin, or Raughlinds, or Raghery, or Rachery,— for in all those different ways is its name written,—is the largest of the islands which lie near the north coast of Ireland, and are considered as a part of it. All the others are small and insignificant, with the exception of Tory or Robber Island, which is of some importance, and is inhabited. There are other ways of writing the name of this island, as Recarn, Recraiu, Raghlin, Rachri, Raclinda. Pliny calls it Ricnia, and Ptolemy Ricinia. I cannot conceive whence all these names have arisen, since the inhabitants themselves, and the neighbours round, call it plainly Rachri, or Rachrin, in which they agree with Hamilton at the close of the last century, and McKenzie still earlier. It is thought that this name is compounded of Ragh Eri (Erin's Fort), which is not improbable, as the Irish have given to several of the islands on their coast names signifying their situation with respect to the mainland; for instance, they call the little island near Dublin, 'Ireland's Eye;' and the insular promontory in Connaught, 'Erin's Head,' (Errishead.) Rathlin consists of two tracts of land, united at a right angle. One of those arms, which runs parallel with the coast of Ireland, is something more than five miles long, and the other about three. In the middle, where the legs of the angle meet, is a bay, at the head of which stand the church of the island, and the seat of the Rector and owner of the island; whence it is called Church Bay. The entire island, as it stands, is the product of a volcanic eruption; the same, no doubt, which formed the opposite coast of Ireland, for the structure of both exactly corresponds. The basis is a white chalky limestone, on which rests a mass of black basalt, which shows itself in Rathlin, as on the coast of Ireland, regularly in a large handsome columnar formation.

The tides and currents, which run near the island, and between it and the mainland, are particularly remarkable. This northern point of Ireland is, in this respect, as remarkable as the south-WestPoint, near Wexford, already mentioned, where, as I have said, some extraordinary phenomena in the motion of the sea take place. As near Wexford, and its promontory Carnsore Point, the tide wave flowing in from the Atlantic ocean, from the west, turns and rushes northwards into the Irish Sea, (according to Boate, the tide of flood runs as far as Dublin, along the coast northwards, and the ebb returns in a southerly direction,) so at the north, near Rathlin, it turns southwards between Ireland and Scotland, and rushes in this direction into the middle of the Irish Sea, while the ebb returns from the south towards the north. The tides thus rushing into the Irish Sea in two different directions, meet in the middle, and, as Boate says precisely enough, come to a stand-still at the harbour of Carlingford, north of Dublin. In this harbour it always flows in from different directions on both sides, and ebbs from it in like manner. As Rathlin, therefore, lies exactly at the vertex of the tidal currents, where the tide rising in the west is first broken and turned southwards, a contest of streams and tides take place here which shows itself in a great eddy, that streams along the whole north coast of Antrim, Derry, and Donegal, as far as Malin Head; so that while the great movement of the principal mass of waters advances from the west to the east, at the same time a stream runs from east to west for some miles along the coast, providing Lough Foyle and the other bays with water. Both streams, the great tide from the west, and the eddy tide from the east, are at the strongest in the narrow strait between the island of Rathlin and Ireland. Beyond Rathlin, the turning point, this eddy ceases; and after turning entirely, the tides, both the principal one and the coast currents, rush in one stream from north to south. From this eddy arise, as Hamilton remarks, many irregularities in the movements of the tides, which he does not seek further to explain, and neither can I, but which agree with those that we have remarked at the south turning-point, near Wexford. Here, as at Wexford, are parts of the coast where it does not flow for six hours, and ebb for six, as it ought; and where the flood and ebb are so irregularly divided, that the one often lasts nine hours and the other but three.

The sailors who navigate round Ireland must always attend to these tides and eddies. A person sailing from Dublin could, if the wind were favourable, arrive at Carlingford, near the county of Down, with the tide coming in from the south; thence he could continue his voyage northwards, with the tide retreating in that direction; and, at the time when the ebb again changes to flood, could arrive at Rathlin, give himself up to the eddy along the coast, and with it sail against the tide westward as far as Malin Head, where the ebb would carry him out into the Atlantic ocean.

The waters between Rathlin and the shore are violently agitated twice a day, even in the calmest weather; that is, at each return of the flood or ebb; and this agitation lasts until the currents have acquired an equal strength, when they rush peacefully by one another, until the setting in of the next change again produces the agitation. So it is in calm weather. But when a storm comes on, the sea is scarcely navigable; and it is not only impossible for the small coasting vessels to make this little voyage, as we have already seen, but even large ships avoid the passage between the island and the mainland. The prevailing winds and waves come, of course, from the open Atlantic ocean, from the west; and therefore the west coast of Rathlin is the scene of immense waves, breaking almost incessantly. In winter, the inhabitants are often, for an entire month, surrounded by furious storms, waves, and tides, isolated from the rest of mankind, and shut out from all intercourse with the mainland.

Such an island was well adapted to afford secure winter quarters to a flying king and his companions. Robert Bruce, king of Scotland, therefore availed himself of all these circumstances when he was compelled, a short time after his coronation, to leave his kingdom in the lurch. In the autumn of the year 1306, he came to Rathlin, with three hundred armed men, and settled himself between the basaltic rocks of the island, behind the breakers, tides, and storms, safe from his persecutors, and remained there through the winter. Crossing over to Scotland in the spring, with increased numbers, he began that varied and eventful war which at last ended with the glorious battle of Bannockburn, in the year 1314, in which Scotland established her freedom, and Bruce secured his kingdom by a victory over the English.

When Bruce landed here, the island was then, as now, inhabited by solitary islanders, tending sheep, catching fish, and cultivating patches of oats. At first they fled before the mail-clad knight to the other side of the island; but when they saw that the iron lord treated them mildly and kindly, they came forward, promised to provide him and his men daily with provisions, fish, mutton, and oat-cakes; and at last, choosing him their lord and king, they appointed themselves his fishers, shepherds, and oat-cake makers, and delivered up to him a castle that had stood from ancient times on their island, and is called 'Bruce's Castle' to this day, while a cavern near it is still called 'Bruce's Cave.' The castle stands on a high promontory, on the east side of the island, within sight of Scotland; and the rock on which it is built rises perpendicularly from the water; but at the present day its ruins consist of nothing but a few walls. On those rocks lived Robert Bruce, with his trusty companions, amongst whom were Sir Robert Boyd, Sir James Douglas, and Angus McDonnell, the sixth 'King of the Isles,' that is, of the islands in the west of Scotland, which formed a separate kingdom dependent upon Scotland, and which bear the same geographical and historical relation to Scotland, that the Ionian islands bear to Greece.

The present successor to Robert Bruce in the government of the island, is a Mr. Gage, who being the spiritual head, the rector, as well as the chief magistrate and the owner of the soil, thus rules his subjects in more relations and by more titles than many a king his kingdom, though he has neither the parade and splendour of sovereignty, nor a prince's crown. This reverend gentleman is a vassal of the Antrim family, from whom his progenitors have held the island, since the year 1740, by lease forever. King Charles I., as I have already stated, made a grant of it to the Antrim family. The head of the Antrim family is still called the 'Chief' of Rathlin. 'The Antrim family holds the Chiefry or Chiefdom,' the people say; but Mr. Gage is called the proprietor; and although he still pays a trifling head-rent to his chieftain, yet the latter has nothing whatever to do with the internal management of the island. The rector's tenants are all only 'at will;' i.e. they can immediately, and without more ado, be deprived by him of their farms and land, and driven from the island.

Mr. Gage might, if he chose, change his residence to Dublin, or some other place, and give up the entire income of his hereditary island to some other person, who would pay him a rent and take the trouble of its management. Such a man would be called by the Irish 'a middleman.' This middleman, to whom the whole island might be leased, would have it in his power to let separate parts of it to under-middlemen, who would then be the immediate landlords of the tenants: thus we should have, from the king to the tenant, a succession of possessors, or at least persons having a title to the soil, one over another, as really happens in an extraordinary number of cases in Ireland. In the first place, there would be the head ruler of all the land, the Queen, to whom all the possessions of the Antrim family would revert under certain circumstances, for instance, should the family become extinct, or should they fail to pay the proper number of falcons due to the Viceroy of Ireland, on the feast of St. John the Baptist. Next, the Antrim family, who reckon the island of Rathlin as part of their earldom, and would take possession of it again, should their vassal not duly pay the chief-rent. Then, the so-called proprietor, Mr. Gage, who lords it here, regulates, rules, and governs, just as he pleases. Then the head-middleman, who might farm the island, under the conditions and articles imposed on him by the proprietor. After him, the under-middlemen, who are connected with the first middleman, and hold their lots from him, as he holds the whole from the proprietor. Of course, under those first middlemen, there may be again a second class; and this is the case on very extensive estates. Lastly, the poor tenants themselves, who are in the end obliged to bear, like a foundation, the entire great feudal structure piled up on them, and whose pence and shillings, scraped up and added together, form the pounds which enable the under-middlemen to satisfy the middleman, and to put something in their own pockets besides; who, moreover, enable the middleman to pay the proprietor, and also to lay by something for himself; who, furthermore, give the proprietor the means of living free from care and in happiness; who increase the splendour of the earl's family; and, in the end, even lend some brilliancy to the jewels of the English crown. If one looks, from the splendour accumulated on the summit, down on the lowly tenants, he may form an idea of their misery and melancholy state of destitution.

The population of the island amounts to about 1100. This number was first accurately determined in the year 1758, when the spiritual chief, and governor of the island, imposed a tax of a shilling on every head, in order with the proceeds to build a new Mass-house, as they term here what in other places people would call a Catholic church. The numbering was accomplished with great trouble; for the islanders opposed it, believing that, out of every numbered family, one individual would surely die. This island also lies under the great injustice which extends all over Ireland, in the relative positions of the Protestants who rule, and the Catholics who are ruled. The rector and owner of the island, who resides here throughout the year with his family, has a good income, and lives in the enjoyment of all imaginable comforts, is a Protestant; but his poor tenants and vassals, from whom he draws this income, and who, in order to be able to pay it, fish, cultivate oats, navigate the stormy sea, and eat seaweed, are poor taxed Catholics, while only sixty or eighty of them are said to be Protestants. For the Catholics, the Protestant rector keeps a Catholic priest, and also, as has been said, keeps a 'Mass-house' in good repair for them. An Irish Protestant, who praised the management of the present rector, thus expressed himself: 'he keeps them (the Catholics) in very good order.' In winter, of course, he lives somewhat solitary, and separated from the rest of the world; but in summer, as he is of a hospitable disposition, he receives many visits from his friends and relations in Ireland and Scotland. His eldest son will succeed him as rector and owner of the island; and his younger son he will find means, by his influence, of advancing to some other benefice in the church. Such is the way in which things are managed in the 'established Episcopal church of Ireland.'

The sheep of Rathlin are much praised: the rocky meadows of the island afford them excellent pasture, and in the north of Ireland they are known by the name of 'Rachries;' a name also given to the islanders themselves, when they cross over to the mainland, where, on account of their rude habits, they appear sometimes to afford considerable merriment to the continentalists of Ireland,—for Ireland naturally stands to Rathlin in the relation of a continent, and all continentalists are accustomed to make themselves merry with the peculiarities of islanders. All these islanders, with the exception perhaps of the Protestants, are said still to speak the ancient Irish language, which is preserved in all the little islands about Ireland, like the Scottish Gaelic, which is even still spoken in greater purity in the kingdom of the Isles than in the rest of Scotland.

The horses of the island are small, being mere 'ponies,' as the people in Ballycastle told me. This is also the case with the horses of the Scottish islands. In the Baltic sea, too, the horses of the island of Gothland are well known and sought after on account of their small size. What can be the cause of the diminutive proportions of island horses? A large horse was once carried over from Ireland to Rathlin, and, as the Ballycastle people say, the islanders took it for a monster, thought it would eat them, and ran away from it.

The only four-footed wild animals belonging to the island, are, according to Hamilton, the rat and the mouse. It is said to contain neither foxes, hares, rabbits, nor badgers, though they are plentiful both in the neighbouring parts of Scotland, and on the coast of Ireland. Foxes are said to have been once introduced into the island by command of a Lord Antrim, and a party of his huntsmen were sent there to form a new hunting-ground; but the islanders, who have a great dislike to this animal, bribed the huntsmen, and induced them to disobey their orders. Lord Antrim, who afterwards became acquainted with this, took occasion therefrom to impose on them a new annual tax, for their immunity from foxes. I believe the people here are very much afraid of those animals; for I happened to hear a woman, whose house I entered the other day, call to her crying child, 'Be silent, or the fox shall catch you.' This might appear comical to African mothers, who probably threaten their children with lions; but the fox is the only beast of prey in England which can conquer a child. In Rachery island, they have nothing but rats for this purpose. In Germany, they generally frighten children with the wolf; in some parts of Russia, where the wolf is too common, they use the bear. Thus from rats, or at least from foxes to lions, there is in this respect a curious ascending scale.

The islanders, as I have already said, cultivate some barley and oats; but besides this, one of their principal sources of gain consists in the preparation of kelp from seaweed, which is the occupation of the women and children. Hamilton thus describes their mode of proceeding:—They gather the seaweed from the shore after a storm, or cut it from the rocks on which it grows, and spread it out in the sunshine to dry. In the evening they gather it into little heaps, which are again spread out to dry next day. When the weeds are dry, they make a hole in the ground, line it with stones, and in this extempore oven burn the weeds slowly and carefully to ashes. The vegetable salts melt, and, falling to the bottom of the hole, form a solid mass, in which state it is exported, as they do not understand how to purify the soda from the common salt and other matters mixed with it. This preparation of kelp, as the English call it, is carried on through the entire north-west coast of Ireland, and in a similar manner on the south-western coasts of Scotland, and it forms a not inconsiderable article of trade with England.

What was told me of the manners of the simple inhabitants of this island, brought to my recollection the inhabitants of some of the islands in the Baltic. Thus it is remarkable, that the same trait is related of the Racheries as of the people of Runoe, in the Gulf of Riga, that the greatest punishment that can be inflicted on them is banishment from their island, which they love exceedingly, regarding Ireland as an altogether foreign country.

We have two accounts, by learned men, of the nature of the island of Raghery: one by Dr. W. Hamilton, in his description of the County of Antrim; and one by Dr. J. Drummond, in the xvii. vol. of the Transactions of the Royal Irish Academy. From the first account I take a few remarks that may perhaps be acceptable to most of my German readers, who may not have the book itself at their command. Small as the island is, two races of very different characters may be discovered among its 1100 inhabitants. The island, as I have already said, consists of two points of land, joined at a right angle. The west, or longer end, is called 'Kenramer,' or, in correct Irish, 'Ceanramber,' i.e. the long end; the other point is called 'Ushet.' Kenramer is rocky and hilly: the little hollows and valleys in it are fertile and well cultivated; but its coast is without a harbour. Ushet, on the other hand, is barren, but more open and accessible, and well supplied with good little havens. The Ushet people are therefore the fishers, sailors, and merchants of the island, who keep up the connection with the mainland, by a lively traffic with the neighbouring market towns of Scotland and Ireland. These Ushet men also generally speak English, and have lost many of their ancient insular peculiarities. The Kenramer men, on the other hand, live independent and shut out on their end of the island, till their fields, and are active climbers of the cliffs. On the north side of their wing, where the rocks rise out at the sea to a height of 750 feet, a great number of sea-fowls build their nests, the robbing of which is their principal employment. A Kenramer man often goes quite alone, provided merely with a rope, on those bird-catching and egg-collecting expeditions. He makes the rope fast at the edge of the cliff, and lets himself down or draws himself up without assistance, as circumstances may require. As they have less communication with strangers, they have preserved their old customs, and the Irish language, more unaltered than the Ushet men. The difference between these two island races is so evident, and they know it so well themselves, that in hard tasks, where the rock-climbers of Kenramer and the seamen of Ushet are employed together, they point out to each other that post for which he is most fitted as an east or west islander.

As the Isle of Man was formerly an apple of discord between England and Scotland, so was Rathlin between Scotland and Ireland. It often served the Scottish and Irish chieftains as the place of meeting and the sallying point of their expeditions. There are therefore many of those tumuli, such as are found in Ireland and Scotland, on a little plain in the centre of the island, which was probably more than once a blood-soaked battle-field. In the centre of one of these tombs, a stone coffin containing bones has been found, while all round were strewn many other human bones, being probably those of a hero, and the common soldiers he commanded. Bronze swords and lance-heads, likewise dug up in this plain, are irrefutable testimonies of the bloody dramas which were performed here. The recollection of the atrocities perpetrated here on one occasion, by the clan of the Campbells, remained so long in the memory of the island population, that so lately as at the end of the last century, no Scotchman of that name was permitted to settle on the island, and this law is probably in force at the present moment. Even in the earliest periods of Irish history, Rathlin is mentioned as an inhabited island; and in the fifth century the Irish and Scotch apostle, St. Columba, founded a monastery here, which, like so many other pious foundations of the kind in Ireland, flourished for three hundred years, till, at the end of the eighth and beginning of the ninth century, the barbarians of the north rushed down and spread themselves over England, Scotland, and Ireland, burying every thing, as in some parts also of France and Germany, and even Italy, in wild destruction, and even swept across the little Rathlin, and laid its pious edifice in ruins.

Cape Fair Head

Basalt Plateau—Farm of the Cross—Little Lakes—A Storm Begets a.Calm—Structure of the Basalt Masses—Rathlin As Seen From Benmore—Dykes in the Basalt—The Gray Man's Path—Substratum of the Basalt—Its Brittleness—Jackstraws—Thick Population—'The Fox is Coming!'—Ideality and Reality

The great masses of basalt which lie upon the original chalk bottom of this part of Ireland, here form a high plateau or table, tolerably flat on the summit, to which one gradually ascends from Ballycastle by a winding road. The highest edge of this plateau is turned towards the sea, whence it inclines inland, with a gentle slope, for about half a mile, when it mixes with other heights and risings of the highlands of the county of Antrim. The inclined surface of this plateau is covered far and wide with grass, moss, and moist boggy soil, and affords pasture for the cattle of a couple of little farms. Next the sea, it ends abruptly in a steep cliff, from four to six hundred feet high, and here the naked black basalt is every where visible. The highest point rises to 636 feet above the level of the sea, and is called Cape Benmore. The visitor drives up as far as a little farm, called the Farm of the Cross, which lies in a hollow immediately behind the Head, where the sloping masses mingle with other hills, and where the waters have collected in two little lakes, of which one is called Lough Dhu, or the Black Lake, and the other Lough Nacrana, or the Lake with the Island. At this farm I had to leave my car, and continue the ascent on foot. The farmer, Patrick Jameson, whose cattle graze on the summit of Benmore, and his servant or neighbour, were our guides. We first went round the little lakes, one of which, Lough Nacrana, is remarkable for a small island in its centre. The farmers told me that the people say that this island was made by the Druids, and used by them in their religious rites. At all events, at least in its present form, it is the work of art; for it rises in a perfectly regular oval form above the surface of the lake, and seems to be built of fragments of basalt, such as lie in vast numbers round the shore of the lake. I have not been able to find any thing respecting this lake and its artificial island in any book, and am willing to believe that the Druids might have chosen this wild spot for the scene of their religious ceremonies. The little farm is the only thing in this wild place that does not remind one of the superhuman works of nature. As Benmore is mentioned by Ptolemeus (it is his *Robogdium*

Promontorium,) it is a proof that it was known and famed as something extraordinary even before the Christian era.

From the little Druidical temple-lake[1], we now ascended to the very top of the cape, by extremely unpleasant paths, for one foot always trod in the wet bog, and the other on pointed rocks. The further we went, however, the more convenient and dry became the path, and above, at the edge of the cliff, it was perfectly level and dry. The storm, too, had somewhat impeded us in our ascent; but when we reached the crown of the hill it ceased completely, and became a perfect calm, which did not move a hair of our heads. This calm at first surprised me not a little, till my guide called my attention to the fact, that the wind struck quite against the perpendicular face of the rock, and was turned off broken, and sent upwards, and consequently produced, not a horizontal current of air, but a vertical one towards the sky. The cliff is so perpendicular, and the edge so sharp, and the wind blew so perfectly at right angles against the wall of rock, that the air immediately behind the up-rushing current was quite still. Further up in the air, the vertical current was, of course, again carried along with the storm from the north; and at a distance of from 500 to 600 paces, the wind again swept along the ground; while still further on, at a distance of 700 or 800 paces, its whole force was felt. The current of air therefore flowed in a great arch over our heads, beneath which we enjoyed a perfect calm.

Basalt, it is well known, is found partly in large, thick, compact, and shapeless masses, which, however, break according to certain laws, assuming certain regular forms. Sometimes, however, basalt is also seen in a certain regular and columnal structure. These columns or pillars are generally as close to each other as if they were cemented together. But wherever the mass has been shattered by violence, or where the basalt is exposed to the air, rain, and other atmospheric influences, these columns are actually seen ranged like pillars. In such places, their joinings open gradually, and the columns are either loosened by time, and fall in long rows, or stand out separated from the walls, or at least show on the surface their outlines somewhat defined by the effects of time. From the completely amorphous basalt masses which have neither an internal

---

[1] Now known to be a *crannóg*, a lake dwelling place, used from Neolithic times to the modern era, which is a convenient retreat and readily defended, [Clachan ed.].

concealed, nor an external apparent structure, to those which show themselves in elegant, perfectly regular, and prettily-formed columns, there are many gradations. Sometimes, the columns of which the entire mass is composed are exceedingly large, thick, and rude, and have no regular and easily recognizable form, while they appear neither circular, nor perfectly four, six, or eight-cornered. They bear the same relation to these elegantly-formed basalt columns, as the vast Cyclopean stones used in the chapel at New Grange do to the elegantly hewn, squared, and polished stones, which a refined and highly developed architecture forms, for its buildings, according to the rules of art. The structure of Fair Head is Cyclopean. There are immense perpendicular columns, like vast numbers of gigantic knotted oaks, rudely and grotesquely fitted together. Most of these mighty pillars stand close together, like the stones of a wall; but some have become half or entirely detached from the mass, and stand out from the wall in low relief, in high relief, or completely apart; and the fate of these last is usually to fall, though one is shown to the stranger which is said to have been standing for centuries, quite separate, and ever threatening to fall. This column is, I think, from thirty to thirty-five feet in circumference, and its head is about ten or twelve feet from the edge of the precipice, and at its sides one looks down into clefts seventy feet deep, which grow narrower and narrower towards the bottom, and contain many overturned pillars, like so many wedges.

On the summit of Benmore Head, we had the nearest promontory of Rathlin Island, Rue Point, exactly opposite us, at a distance of about four miles. The eastern side of this promontory is formed of columnar basalt, like the structure of Benmore Head. Perhaps these two columnar shores were once connected, and were torn asunder by some violent convulsion of nature. The long coast of the western, or Kenramer wing of Rathlin was so clearly visible, that we could see the Church Bay most distinctly, and distinguish the districts of Kenramer and Ushet.

A mountain was shown to us as the site of King Bruce's Castle; and the high chalk cliffs, with their cap of basalt, we saw with such distinctness as to be able to study their structure. I could scarcely persuade myself that it was not possible to reach this island, so near did it appear to us, or that in winter it lay as unconnected with Ireland as if it were a hundred miles off. But from our observatory we saw the foam of the wild breakers that made it unapproachable. My guides told me that a storm was almost constantly blowing on Rathlin, so that no trees could grow high in the rector's garden. As soon as they grew higher than the garden wall they sickened and died. There are, therefore, none larger than bushes on the island.

In the middle, between Rathlin and the coast of Ballycastle, a speck was pointed out to me, caused, as was said, by the meeting of seven tides. The sailors call this point Slough na Moran. It is a whirlpool, produced by the meeting of the ebbing and flowing tides, and eddies and counter-eddies, assisted perhaps by submarine rocks.

While contemplating Rathlin island, and Bruce's Castle, I thought of Shakspere's Tempest, and the island of the banished duke Prospero. Might it not be possible that Shakspere, who doubtless had heard of Bruce and Rathlin, took from this event in Bruce's life his idea of making a lonely island, the abode of a banished prince, the scene of a drama? The wild inhabitants whom Bruce took into his service, are represented by Caliban. Shakspere only transferred his island to the sunny south, which is most suited for lively dramatic action and poetry. Here, in the cold, dull, windy north, hover only the lyric cloud-forms of Ossian's heroes.

As the traveller ascends the basaltic mass of Benmore Head, he perceives several hollows in the mass, beginning at the edge of the precipice, and running inland, parallel to one another. The farmers of the neighbourhood had here and there bordered them with walls of loose stones, and used them, they said, as boundaries for their fields, and enclosures for their cattle. These hollows are caused by great fissures or clefts, which stretch from the shore far inland, and are again filled with basalt. As they were either not completely filled, or the filling substance was less enduring than the chief mass, these dykes, as the English term them, are still perceptible on the surface. Wherever the filling material has again fallen out of these dykes or fissures, there are wide clefts. One of these, on Benmore Head, is used by the inhabitants of the coast as a regular passage down to the sea. This path they call Fhir Leith, or 'the Gray Man's Path.' The Gray Man, who is almost ceaselessly travelling this path, is the storm. The wind that rushes up from it is so strong, that, the instant I set foot in it, my cloak, hat, books, and maps were whipped away into the air, like the water we saw yesterday spouting up from similar clefts. The Gray Man amused himself for some time in playing with these trifles, till we snatched them from him again, and hid them behind a lofty basalt column.

A vast and mighty column has fallen right across the Gray Man's Path, and is fixed like a wedge between its walls, yet leaving room enough to pass beneath it. One cannot avoid hastening past it, for it looks as if it were about to fall still farther. But it has been meditating this fall from time immemorial, and many generations have passed through uncrushed. At the top, the fissure is very narrow, being only eight or ten feet wide; but it becomes wider towards the bottom. Mighty columns are ranged along on either side; but in the fissure itself they are broken off, so that one can step from the head of one to that of another, and descend as if on a flight of irregular stairs. The heads of these broken pillars are almost all flat, and afford a tolerably level surface, on which one can occasionally sit down to rest, as on a stone seat. These columns do not all consist of one piece, but are composed of a number of blocks, placed one over another. The separate blocks are not, however, always easily distinguishable, because they are very firmly and closely fitted together; but when the columns fall, these joinings open, and they divide into the pieces of which they were originally composed. The component blocks of the pillars of Fair Head are, I think, from ten to fifteen feet long, while the entire columns are from 200 to 250 feet in height. We shall afterwards see that when the columns are most elegantly formed these blocks are shorter and smaller.

The entire weight of this stratum of columnar basalt, 250 feet thick, rests on a bed of clay-slate (Thonschieferlage), which again rests on a substratum of stone coal. This is the reverse of what we might expect; for the heavy, almost indestructible, iron-hard basalt, ought properly to lie beneath, and the brittle clay-slate and coal strata to rest upon it. The basalt columns owe their frequent falls to the brittleness and unenduring nature of the clay-slate which forms their foundation. The joinings of the columns also assist these falls; for the water which penetrates them in the autumn being frozen in the winter, it enlarges the fissures with irresistible force, till at length, after centuries of unobserved toil, they become so wide, the substratum of clay-slate so crumbled away, and the pillars overhang so much, that they lose their balance, topple over some stormy winter's night, when all the elements are in uproar, and are dashed into hundreds and thousands of fragments, and partly ground to dust amid the roaring breakers. As the stratum of clay-slate upon which the columnar basalt rests is 400 feet above the sea, it must be a wonderful and dread-creating spectacle, when these giants dash themselves from their lofty pedestals, and make their *salto mortale*[1] into the depths beneath. Besides, this cannot happen without the production of electricity and fire, since the basalt is so hard that it throws off sparks when lightly struck against another hard body. The fall therefore must be accompanied with flashes of fire and showers of sparks. Yet no human eye has ever beheld this spectacle in its full magnificence, often as it has been enacted. Almost all these wild sports of nature can only be seen with fancy's eye, since danger and terror usually drive man from their neighbourhood. To see them, one should be able to float above them, like a bird.

Below, where the Gray Man's Path ceases, and the substrata of clay-slate and coal begin, all is covered with ruins, with blocks of columns, with fragments of rock, big and little, with entire pillars, and portions of pillars. In Germany, and also in France and England, there is a game called Lenorchen[2] in some parts of Germany. A number of finely divided little sticks are thrown together on the table, so that they lie across and beneath and leaning and resting upon each other, as chance placed them, and the task assigned to the players is, cautiously to remove the little splinters, one by one, without touching or shaking the others. Here, in the lower regions of Fair Head, it looks as if a party of Titans had been playing at this game with columns of basalt, for the pillars and fragments of pillars are heaped upon one another in every possible direction. Here and there many lie together, and look like the ruins of some great and noble building; sometimes they lie in a mass, horizontally, one upon the other. One might imagine that the giants had collected a parcel of Egyptian pyramids, obelisks, Pompey's-pillars, Stephen's-towers, and castle walls, to play a game of jackstraws with them. It is fortunate for travellers that they no longer play at them, and that, though apparently so loose, yet in fact they are all so firm that one can climb over them without fear. Many blocks have fallen into the sea, and the waves dash high above them into the clefts, fissures, holes, and breaches. Remarkable and grand from below is the view of the great arch of columns, which adorns the brow of the promontory, like a mural crown on the head of a Roman citizen. The vast cleft of the Gray Man, seen from here, looks like a line or a small chink in the immense mass; and the pillar across it, which, when above, one expects to fall every

---

[1] deadly fall, [Clachan ed.].
[2] Called 'Jackstraws' in England.—[tr.]

99

moment, is here scarcely distinguishable from the rest, and not the least of its threatening aspect is visible. Though the wind helped us up the Gray Man's Path, it took us not quite an hour to reascend from the surf to the top of the rock. We found our chattels behind the pillar, and I took my dinner in the cabin of my Benmore herdsman. It consisted of whisky, oat-cakes, and four fried eggs. The hostess had a whole crowd of children around her, like most Irish mothers, who are every where very prolific, even on these barren basalt headlands. In Germany, only the fine and fertile tracts are thickly inhabited, and sometimes over-inhabited; but in Ireland, even the turf-bogs and the rocks are crowded with inhabitants, as if human beings were here hatched, like the wild sea-fowl, by hundreds and thousands, in the clefts and fissures of the rocks. Even the little island of Rathlin, with its 1100 inhabitants, is said to contain twice too many. The Catholic priests are partly to blame for this over-population, for they are the most busy match-makers in Ireland. As a chief part of their income is derived from marriages, they are most anxious to unite young people as soon as they are marriageable. If the Roman Catholic clergy were chosen from a higher class, were better paid, and their social position improved, this eagerness for marriage-making would probably cease, and the surplus population of Ireland no longer pressing so heavily on the country, one great source of the misery of the land would be removed.

'Go a one side, the fox is coming!' cried the farmer's wife to the little squallers, when they were going to make away with the eggs and oat-cakes intended for me; and thus, with the fox's aid, I at last got something warm to assuage my hunger, although I did not allow the little brood to remain quite so hungry as they had previously been. The children did not understand a word of Irish, but all spoke English, though their mother spoke Irish from her youth. 'The young people are all going out of the Irish,' said she. Thus even here in the Glynns—to which district Fair Head also belongs—the English is yearly and daily gaining new victories over the Irish. These people, like most of the inhabitants of the Glynns, were Catholics. On the other side of the river, at Ballycastle, Protestantism again begins. 'There they are all in the Presbyterian way,' said the farmer, 'like the haland (highland) people.' The weather formed our chief topic of conversation, over our turf-fire,—how severe and disagreeable it was now; how beautiful it had been five days ago; then how this 'terrible break down' had come all at once, and how the weather would soon mend again. All the time I was reflecting how nearly the cottage and the palace resemble each other with respect to conversation on the weather, which is a topic not to be avoided any where on the wide circle of the entire world. In the afternoon I returned to tea to my Misses McDonnell. 'Well, have you been satisfied?' 'Have you been greatly disappointed?' were the questions that met me. 'It usually happens that travellers on our coast return disappointed from their excursions.'

'You are right,' replied I; 'I too have heard of travellers being disappointed with your coast; but I must confess, I consider these men either as persons totally incapable of appreciating the wonders of nature, or as blasé, who assume an air of importance, and wish people to understand that Nature, with all her mighty works, is mere child's-play compared with the pictures their own imaginations are able to create. It is in some measure true, however, that the creations of Nature actually fall short of those of the imagination. I, for instance, can imagine columns, 20,000, instead of 250 feet high, with the fleecy clouds floating about their summits. I can imagine these columns in every possible position, oblique or perpendicular, and divided into stories like a house, so that we can mount from landing-place to landing-place, as in the interior of a tower. We can imagine that Nature has built arches of rock, ten or twenty times as high as the gateway of the Colossus of Rhodes; and that she has placed thousands of such arches, beside and upon one another, in rows, like those of a Roman amphitheatre. Is it not possible, moreover, to imagine, in the middle of a plain, a hole that yawns with a gorge half a mile in diameter, quite round, and six or twelve miles deep? By means of natural steps, one can descend on a two days' journey into this hole, and then, looking up as from an enormous well, contemplate the stars of heaven from the neighbourhood of the centre of the earth.'

'What cannot the imagination do with ice! Picture to yourself this beautiful crystal-like substance, of the clearest, purest transparency, and now let your uncurbed fancy build out of it a palace, worthy of standing at the North Pole for the ice-king. Heaven-high columns of greenish ice; beautiful arches, great and small, thrown from column to column, spring so high that the clouds, gilded by the sun, sport in play from capital to capital. The ice must be clean, and not covered with snow or mud, as in Switzerland; and in the night-time the Aurora Borealis may dance and glisten around it, and here and there shimmer through its transparent walls. And yet no such thing exists in nature.'

'Many other incredibly splendid and magnificent spectacles we may imagine, such as may possibly exist on the wild moon, or on some other still ruder planet. All men, I believe, do this more or less; for we have all more or less of this magic power we call fancy or imagination within us. We try the phenomena of Nature by the standard of our air-castle building fancy, and are then dissatisfied with the reality. Do we remain, however, within our human limits—do we visit, in the modest consciousness of our weakness, those scenes which exceed all the powers as well of the mind as of the body, they cannot fail to make a mighty impression upon us. From this point of view, and not in comparison with Utopian things, which may perhaps exist on other planets, but with those which actually exist here on earth, I must say that your Benmore is unquestionably one of the most wonderful, magnificent, and remarkable things any one can behold.'

The Irish are all very desirous that the traveller should be satisfied with every thing in their fatherland, and that he should bestow becoming admiration on every thing. They are fond of hearing the praises of the traveller, and they expect them. This is because they seldom see travellers in their country, and therefore feel themselves honoured by their visits, as well as because they are most friendly towards strangers, and, as it were, enamoured of their fatherland. The Misses McDonnell, therefore, who had been anxiously waiting my return, were content with my report, and retired to bed perfectly gratified.

The Giant's Causeway

Next day I set out for the Giant's Causeway. The wind was still blowing and roaring from the north, with the same violence as it now had for some days. It dashed against the steep, rugged cliffs, it howled skywards up the rocks, in immense arches it again descended on the road I was travelling, and in long-drawn, lofty waves, greater probably than all the waves ever formed on an ocean of water, it billowed along through the ocean of the atmosphere; for though all these currents of the air were less visible and perceptible than the corresponding commotions of the waters, they nevertheless existed for all that. On the coast I observed many 'puffing-holes,' such as I have above described, from which the water spouted up as if from the nostrils of a whale. My equipage was again a little Irish one-horse car, and my soul was full of what I was to see. As the rocks of the whole coast of Antrim are covered with ruins, the remains of old castles from that heroic period which the Irish and Scottish ballads still glorify, there are, immediately behind Ballycastle, the ruins of two, called Dunning and Kenbaan Castles. Both are situated on a lofty limestone rock, that rises abruptly from the sea. On the left side of the road are seen the traces of a still older work of man; the remains of the Round Tower of Armoy. Wherever it was possible, we dismounted and examined every thing, to the annoyance of our driver and his horse, whose patience we tried severely.

In the immediate vicinity of the valley of Ballycastle there seems to be nothing but limestone. The strangest forms show themselves where the basalt again makes its appearance, and the first extraordinary, interesting point is Carrick-a-Rede, as English orthography writes it, or Caraig-a-Ramhad, according to the proper Irish spelling, i.e. the rock on the road.

Properly speaking, there are two rocks, formed of two masses of basaltic columns, clustered closely together, each about 200 feet high, with a circumference of some thousands of feet. The one is connected with the mainland by a little isthmus; but the other is pushed out completely into the sea, and separated from the other by a deep chasm. A little island that lies not far from it is called Sheep Island. Even to the Faroe Islands (Sheep Islands) this is a very usual appellation for such islands as afford pasturage for sheep only. Many of these small 'Sheep Islands' also lie along the Scottish coast. The fresh, green, grassy summit of this little island contrasts agreeably with the black basalt pillars which support it.

In summer, the island is connected with the headland by a bridge, made in the following manner. Two thick ropes are, by some expert climbers, fastened to two iron rings, which have been driven into the rocks at each side. These ropes are then connected by little cross-ropes, upon which small boards are laid. A third rope, fastened a little higher than the other two, serves as a handrail. This slender bridge, which is more than sixty feet long, swings of course with every step, and sways to and fro in the wind over the abyss; but the people assured me that even their wives, with their children in their arms, cross it without fear or difficulty. In the autumn it is removed, lest the ropes might be lost in some storm; and unfortunately this operation had been performed before our visit, and the island was, for us, inaccessible. Nevertheless, sheep were grazing on it, and, as the people told me, remain there the entire winter, never wanting for food, and finding shelter behind the rocks and in some caves. When the shepherd requires to visit them, he must do so by means of a boat. This bridge is probably one of the oldest suspension-bridges in the British dominions. Many similar constructions are to be found on the Scottish and Irish coasts, where it is the usual means by which two rocks are connected which can be communicated with in no other way. In fact, it is remarkable that this system of suspension-bridges should have been here in such general use, and constructed by simple fishermen and shepherds, before the thinking heads and great inventors of Britain thought of applying it on a grand scale, and using it for the improvement of intercourse on the great lines of trade.

The picture presented by these two rocks of Carrick-a-Rede, with the little black island beside them, is surprisingly beautiful. We were obliged to be content with enjoying it from the shore, where we chose a spot, sheltered by a grass-covered basalt wall, whence we could see it as plainly as if we were sitting in the very middle of it. The mighty breakers ceaselessly rushed against the island, sending their high-dashing foam even to the sheep on its summit. On the side of the island, turned towards us, was a little bay, shut in by high rock-walls, so that it lay like a mirror unruffled by the slightest breath of air; and this although the storm was raging close beside it. In this bay, and in the little strait between the rocks and the island, the people carry on a not-unimportant salmon-fishery in the summer; for as the salmon come in the spring time from the open sea to deposit their spawn in the bays and mouths of rivers, they usually coast along the shore, searching for the sweet water, and linger in the little strait between Carrick-a-Rede and the mainland, and in the quiet bay of the former. The fishermen take their measures accordingly, and have also built a small hut on the low shore of the bay for their convenience. The salmon-fishery of the entire north of Ireland is of great importance, and quantities of salmon have, from time immemorial, been exported thence to the markets of Spain and Italy.

Proceeding along the coast, we again got a view of an old ruin, which lies on the extremity of a mass of rocks, projecting far into the sea. It was Castle Dunseverick, said to have been built by an ancient Irish king, Sobhairee, 800 years before the birth of Christ! These castles, on island-rocks, surrounded by the brawling sea, are quite peculiar to the northern coast of Ireland. The most remarkable, largest, and most beautiful of all these castles is that of Dunluce, near the Giant's Causeway. Dunseverick is said to be one of the three oldest castles in Ireland, (the two others of equal antiquity are Dunkarmna and Cahirconry). An Irish king, Rotheacht, was struck by lightning on this rock; and it was once besieged by the Danes, with a fleet of 200 ships. Many Irish families trace their descent from Milesius, through the builder of Dunseverick Castle.

We perceived, by the number of persons who soon surrounded us, offering their services, that we were at last approaching the great work of nature which was the object of our journey. As, in Ireland, there are always a dozen men where one only is requisite, there were here also a crowd of men, old and young, well-clad and in rags, all of whom represented themselves as the best guides for the Giant's Causeway.

'Take me, your honour,' cried one: 'I showed Field-Marshal Mac Donald the Giant's Causeway, when he came to visit Ireland, and his own country, Scotland.'

'Take me, your honour,' shouted another: 'I showed every bit of the Giant's Causeway to his Grace the Duke of Wellington, and his Grace was exceedingly well pleased with me.'

'And I, your honour,' said a third, 'have a certificate from the Most Noble the Marquis of Anglesea, and his lady and his daughter.'

'Sir,' boasted a fourth, 'I am the best friend of Professor Buckland, of Oxford, who said that every thing I told him of the Giant's Causeway was perfectly true, and I can show your honour every stone of it.'

I chose the one who seemed to have the most promising physiognomy, and, in fact, I was not deceived in him. I was, however, greatly deceived in imagining, that, after I had proclaimed my election, the rest would leave me in quietness. No such thing. According to the obtrusive custom of their country, the entire troop followed me every step of the way. At first I conjured them to remain at home, and not to disturb my enjoyment of the sublime work of nature, with their unnecessary chattering. I entreated them, I gave them money, I supplicated them, I cursed them,—all in vain. They hunted me, as dogs would a deer; and I was at last obliged to yield to my fate, and make peace with them. One party collected stones for me; another pulled me by the right arm to show me this; while another pulled me by the right to show me that. I do not exaggerate a tittle. In summer, one fares somewhat better; for as many strangers are then usually there at the same time, the guides of course divide their favours between them. But as I was now the only visitor, I had the whole tribe together in my train. In the vicinity of the Giant's Causeway, amid the cultivated fields on the high coast-land, is a large new hotel, where I left my car and entered, while my pursuers remained waiting for me at the door; and when, after taking some refreshment, I again made my appearance, the chase immediately recommenced.

The distance is not far, and the Giant's Causeway is soon gained. 'Causeway,' as is well known, means a high paved road, thrown up like a dam or embankment. The strangest thing about this Giant's Causeway is, that at first sight it seems as if people had erred in naming it; and it looks as if it should properly be called the Dwarf's Causeway. It might be appropriately called Giant's Causeway if it were of vast length, or stretched out for several miles into the sea. But it is not longer than 700 feet, which may be considered extremely short, in comparison with the usual length of roads. It is nothing more than the beginning of a causeway, which soon after sinks beneath the waves of the sea. One might, at the first glance, be inclined to ask himself, why all his attention and anxiety on account of this world-famous word, was directed merely to the little portion of this wide and magnificent coast to which this title is pre-eminently applied; but after he has looked about a little, after he has more closely inspected the Causeway itself and its parts, and especially after he has endeavoured to meditate on it, and to ask himself the how and the why it was made, all his contempt for it vanishes immediately, and the warmest admiration takes its place, yea, the most decided enthusiasm, for this wondrous, inconceivable, mysterious, and in every sense unsurpassingly charming, work of nature.

Yet before my readers can sympathise with this enthusiastic admiration of mine, I must communicate to them as much as I can concerning the formation and structure of this coast. I have already said that, at Benmore, the basalt appears in a vast stratum, 250 feet thick, falling into massy, mighty Cyclopean pillars. Here, at the Giant's Causeway, it is different. In its neighbourhood, on the right and on the left, from Benmore Head to the mouth of the river Bush, a distance of about three miles, the basalt exhibits itself on the rugged shore in the following manner. Not one thick stratum, but many, though mostly two, are plainly distinguishable all along the above-mentioned line of coast. Between the two basalt-strata is a bed of ochre, which again appears beneath the lower strata of basalt, and is then followed by clay-slate, coal, and other substances. It therefore seems as if, here at least, fluid basalt had been twice poured over the entire country, and that in the interval another substance had been deposited on the first layer of basalt. As the basalt strata are every where quite concealed from the eye, and show themselves only along the precipitous rugged shores, where they are split into numerous columns, and appear like a long row of pillars, the word colonnade might in this respect be justly used to describe their appearance. The columns of the first colonnade, beginning from the sea, are, on an average, about fifty-four feet high; but the second has columns about sixty feet long. Hamilton speaks of pillars only thirty feet high; but these measures have been given me by a gentleman at Belfast, who has bestowed much attention to the study of this coast. It is next to impossible to decide this; for the two colonnades are by no means every where of an equal height: sometimes the pillars are more broken off; sometimes they seem to be partly or entirely concealed from the eye by ochre, or by some other substance being deposited before them. The uncovered colonnades, however, which can be traced along the entire coast above-mentioned, come near the average height I have given above. The basalt pillars are all perpendicular; but the ochre, and other strata beneath them, have a sloping surface, as is plainly evident in the profile of the projecting points and headlands of the coast.

I must next remark, that the two colonnades do not every where rest on an horizontal bed, and are not equi-distant from the surface of the sea. They sometimes descend to the surface of the sea, and again rise high above it, so that it looks as if the fluid basalt had spread itself like a cloth over the original inequalities of the ground. At last the colonnades are lost by sinking down beneath the surface of the sea, where they either cease altogether, or are continued beneath it—first, the lower colonnade; and then, near the mouth of the river Bush, the upper. Where this second or upper colonnade or pillar-stratum reaches the surface of the sea, all the other materials, and ochre and clay strata, which rest upon columns, are removed, and the naked pavement formed by the heads of the basaltic pillars is exposed; and this part forms what is called the Giant's Causeway. The descent of the first colonnade beneath the sea probably produces something similar; yet this circumstance is wanting, viz. that the heads of the pillars are not so beautifully bare and exposed to the light of day. A second irregularity of these rows of pillars is, that they are often broken by great gaps or dykes, such as I have already described. These dykes or gaps, which sometimes run through all the strata of the coast, are manifestly of later origin. They must have been made when every thing already lay in the order in which we now see it. They are usually filled with basalt; but the most curious part is, that the basalt in them is sometimes composed of layers of horizontal pillars. At the same time, together with these dykes, there often occurs a depression or vertical displacement of both the strata and the columns. Such a depression is even sometimes found unaccompanied by a dyke; and this the English call 'a fault.' It looks as if an entire piece of the coast had sunk down, with all its strata.

Finally, there are two principal strata or rows of columns every where to be seen; but they are by no means every where the only ones. On the contrary, other parcels of pillars here and there peep up out of the lower or intervening strata; and if these are not as handsome and regularly formed colonnades, there is at least a variety of lower or higher steps or ranges of basalt between them. There are also, of course, between the colonnades, strata entirely composed of mere amorphous basalt or ochre. In the ochre are seen some streaks of iron ore, and in the basalt is a stratum of coal. Here and there, little strata of clay, resembling Puszuolan earth, make their appearance.

The wonderful structure of the columns themselves can no where be studied and admired better than at the Giant's Causeway, where the most beautiful and most regular specimens lie exposed to the inquiring geologist. By far the greater number of the columns are hexagonal. From this hexagonal shape we may conclude that the pillars were all at one period long, soft shafts, which, from being strongly pressed against one another, were of necessity forced to assume the hexagonal form; just as the cells of bees, or any other round body, when pressed equally on all sides by similar bodies. All these columns, however, could become hexagonal without an exception, only under the supposition that all the round shafts were of perfectly equal thickness, and the pressure on all sides equally strong. But as neither was the case, there also arose irregular hexagons, with unequal sides; and then pillars were formed with three, four, five, seven, eight, and nine sides: three and four-sided, when the wide sides of several hexagons met together; seven, eight, and nine-sided, when a thick pillar happened to stand amid many narrow sides of several hexagons. Those with seven and five sides are frequent, but eight-sided pillars are rare, and only one with nine sides has been found. Perfect hexagons, mathematically equilateral, are not often met with. The pillars, of course, do not stand loosely beside one another, but are firmly pressed and cemented together, so that it requires considerable force to separate them.

The diameter of the pillars at the Causeway is from a foot to a foot and a quarter: these are, accordingly, the thinnest and most elegant basaltic columns that are found. There are, it is true, still smaller basaltic crystallizations, with a diameter of a few inches. I myself found, in a dyke, a multitude of little prisms, with three and four sides; but they are far from being so regularly and elegantly formed as the larger pillars at the Causeway, which, on the whole, are the most perfect of their kind. Those little prisms, as the guides assured me, are seldom found any where else but in the dykes, in which I saw them lying loosely on one another. If we consider the entire pillars, first, relative to their position, independent of their combination and structure, we will find here too an exceedingly remarkable phenomenon, governed by a tolerably constant rule, not that this rule admits of no exception. I say remarkable phenomenon; for it might be imagined, that, in this crystallization of a dead inanimate body, every thing should go on according to strict and most unalterable laws, and that one should be shaped exactly like the other. The rule is, that all the pillars stand perpendicularly: all the thousands and thousands of columns of the Giant's Causeway are perfectly upright; and only where a breach has been made, where a piece has been thrown down, are they to be found oblique, and in every possible variety of position. But in other places in the vicinity of the Causeway, many pillars have a naturally inclining position, which they must have assumed when the entire mass was still in a soft, yielding condition. I have already mentioned that the pillars in the dykes sometimes lie in an horizontal position. At Ushet, in Rathlin island, a great quantity of pillars lie in an originally slanting posture. At the promontory of Doon Point, on the same island, and not far from the ruins of Dunseverick, they form a multitude of regular curves, and look like bent down fir trees, as if they were not fluid enough to flow into one another, but yet soft enough to bend over, and then to have hardened in this bowed position. On this island, others are in an horizontal position, and this too in every possible direction, either parallel with the coast, so as to show their whole length, or running into the hill, with their extremities only sticking out.

In fine, on a promontory, near the Giant's Causeway, are to be seen pillars of a waving form, of which the wave-lines or bendings are at the same time perfectly parallel to one another. It looks as if a giant had taken the mass of yet soft pillars, and had bent them a couple of times across his knee. As the irregularly bent figures cannot be explained by the laws of crystallization, which only produce regular and straight lines, we must suppose that, while the basalt was still soft, something occurred externally which caused this peculiarity of form. While it was in this soft state, other stones may perhaps have been dashed against it or pressed down upon it, and the positions of the columns are even now sometimes altered by the operation of similar causes. All these things are, in fact, very wonderful, and, when we consider them more closely, inconceivable. Almost still more astonishing, however, is the construction of the columns taken singly. They consist, not of one single piece, but are built up of a multitude of small blocks called joints, which lie regularly upon one another, like stones in a well-built wall. The joints adhere to each other merely by compression, without any cement, and, as it seems, more firmly than the pillars to one another, so that not the least trace of these joints is perceptible outside, and it requires great force to divide a pillar into the several portions of which it is composed.

I have already remarked, in the description of Fair Head, that the coarse rude pillars are there composed of joints and blocks, and that these blocks seemed to be from eight to ten feet long. In the more elegant columns of the Giant's Causeway and its vicinity, the blocks are usually not more than from six to eight or twelve inches high or thick, so that a pillar of thirty feet high may consist of nearly forty portions. There are even joints which are but four inches thick; and others, on the contrary, which are two or three feet, or even longer. It is a very remarkable circumstance connected with these joints, that the chink or break which separates them does not go quite through, but that at every corner there is a little piece of basalt which is not broken or jointed, and which passes from one block to the other, fastening them more firmly together, like a cramp-iron. The people in the neighbourhood call these cramping-pieces 'spurs' and they are as little visible on the outside as the seams of the joints. I cannot describe the regular form of these spurs. Sometimes they may not exist at all; but that they are generally present is evident, among other reasons, from this, that the labourers at the Giant's Causeway assert that they cannot divide any pillar into its natural joints without first breaking off the spurs, which will not break in the middle. For this purpose, they first strike with a hammer the corners of the prism, in the spot where they suppose the two joints meet, and when the spur is thus removed, they then break off the block itself. In many pillars, Nature has herself undertaken the removal of the spurs; and there are, here and there on the coast, columns which appear, not like regular six or seven-sided prisms, but like a series of more or less irregularly shaped blocks, piled one on another. The sides of the joints are not flat, but a little convex or concave. This convexity and concavity is, however, very slight, being about half an inch in height or depth, sometimes perhaps a little more. The convexity of one pillar always fits most accurately into the corresponding concavity of its neighbour, and the one gains a complete impression of the other, to the very smallest details. These concavities and convexities are, of course, of greater or less circumference, so that all parts of the six or seven-sided prism do not always share in the convexity or concavity. On the contrary, they are usually somewhat flat at the edge or circumference. It usually happens, that, when a

---

joint is concave on its upper surface, it is convex on its lower, or vice versa. But there are also many joints either convex or concave on both surfaces; and, finally, concavity and convexity sometimes completely disappear, and the joints rest on flat surfaces. All these things show themselves in some pillars of the Giant's Causeway with astonishing regularity. The blocks are so firmly united, the concavities are so neatly formed, the sides of the neighbouring pillars fit so closely together, that one might suppose that Finn Mac-Cul, the giant who erected this structure, used a microscope to see that every thing was accurately formed and closely fitted.

Such is the structure of the coast, the arrangement and order of the columns, the composition of each individual pillar. Let us go a step farther, and consider a single pillar-joint by itself, without regard to the manner of its connection with the others. Here, also, new wonders make their appearance, for a spheroidal structure of every individual joint becomes apparent on close examination. In general, the mass of which they are composed is so compact that this structure is not perceptible. But the removal of the spurs, which takes off the angle of the prisms, indicates an inclination of the blocks to assume a spheroidal form, for it is the first step towards making it round. In many blocks we can go still further than the striking off the spurs, and, by regularly hewing off spheroidal layers, may make the block more and more round, till at last we arrive at a tolerably round kernel in the centre. On examination of the external surfaces of the above-described concavities and convexities, we also perceive radial lines, running from the centre of the concavity to the circumference, somewhat like those lines seen on the surface of a leaden bullet, flattened against a wall. All this would lead us to suppose that the entire mass of the Giant's Causeway, and of the other columnar strata in the neighbourhood, originally consisted of a vast multitude of spherical bodies, which were at first soft, and, from being compressed on all sides, thus naturally assumed the form of hexagonal prisms and blocks. This is its appearance; that this compression and joining of the spheroids did not, however, take place from without, but that it was caused by a splitting, dividing, and formation of the mass from within, outwards, according to the mysterious laws of crystallization, is indeed more than probable. The supposition of a pressure from without would not be sufficient perfectly to explain all the phenomena; for as this pressure would have had a greater effect on the external strata of pillars or spheroids than on the internal, the external would unquestionably be pressed flatter, while the internal would have retained a more spherical shape, which is contrary to the fact. It is not necessary, however, that the prismatic blacks should have actually had an internal spheroidal structure, conjointly with an external globular form. Were this the case, we might indeed suppose that they had also lost it again by pressure. But they may have had a tendency to a globular form without being able to arrive at that form, because each disturbed and hindered its neighbour in attaining this. As in a freezing mass of oil, an innumerable multitude of little globules are formed, which, by degrees, are united into one firm mass of ice, so in the cooling mass of basalt, acted upon throughout by the powerful electric and magnetic forces of crystallization, we may imagine a multitude of little globules to have been produced, which continued to increase in size till at length they mutually prevented each other's growth, and consequently assumed the form of hexagonal prisms. In this whirl and commotion of the component globules of the entire mass, many may have separated themselves from it completely; and in fact, as my friend, Dr. Bryce, of Belfast, informed me, perfectly round pieces of basalt, composed of several coatings or layers, like pearls, are found in the superincumbent stratum. They are imbedded in the ochre, and their outer coating presents a kind of transition between basalt and ochre.

All this explanation, as well as every other, however profound, properly comes to nothing. For while we are still as far as ever from discovering the cause by which these phenomena have been produced, even the most superficial inspection of the basaltic pillars suggests so many questions that one scarcely ventures to utter them. But in all investigations concerning inscrutable subjects of this kind, we derive at least this advantage, that we learn their inscrutability, and are the more plainly convinced of the unfathomable depths of that mystery which envelopes all things, even those that lie before our eyes so clear and tangible. We here see before us the most precise and obvious effects of the operation of causes which are completely beyond the reach of our inquiries. This remark is, indeed, more or less applicable to every work of nature; but in such gigantic works as the Giant's Causeway these considerations and feelings present themselves still more powerfully, because the stupendous phenomenon here exhibits itself so clearly before our eyes. We walk on the heads of 40,000 gracefully-formed columns (for at this number the mere pavement of the Causeway has been computed), and all these pillars are as neatly wrought as if they had been polished by the hand of man. They are so regularly composed, of such elegant pieces, every thing fits so well, and the whole structure is so judiciously and fitly supported, that we might suppose it could only be accomplished by the ingenuity of men; and yet it was the hidden forces of nature, acting according to unchangeable laws, that shaped it thus, apparently without having any particular object in view; and what laws these were, must to all eternity remain beyond the ken of human understandings. Even the most common-place questions are still enveloped in the thick gloom of uncertainty; for we do not know how far these columns extend beneath the sea, and as little do we know how far they run into the land, which covers them with a veil as impenetrable as that of the sea, A geologist must many a time long to transform himself into a mole, to creep into the chinks and crannies of the strata, or into a fish, to be able to fathom the depths of the ocean.

The beauty, accuracy, and, I may say, the care, with which the columns of the Giant's Causeway have been wrought by these obscure, objectless, chance powers, are what especially produce so strong, and even sympathizing and loving admiration for this great masterpiece of nature. I had to touch the columns, and to feel their smooth surfaces, before I could believe what my eyes saw; and so was it with me afterwards, whenever I beheld pillars from the Giant's Causeway in other places. Many columns have been raised, broken into their component blocks, and set up in the gardens or the mansions of the neighbouring districts. In many of the extensive parks and gardens of Belfast, Derry, and the north of Ireland generally, as well as in Scotland and in most museums of England, one meets with basalt blocks from the Causeway, built up into columns. Whenever I again saw these pillars in such gardens, I felt myself drawn towards them, and, as it were, by some magnetic influence, was compelled to touch, to take the heavy blocks asunder, and to fit them together again. So much for the external form, position, combination, and texture of the basalts of the Giant's Causeway, which, though they are found in the basalts of other parts of the world, are yet no where either so beautiful and regular, nor so numerous and extensive.

Even in the chemical composition of the material, there is as great variety as in the form. Thus, for instance, the basalts in the dykes I have mentioned have partly altered the composition of the earthy strata through which they run, and have been themselves partly altered where they come in contact with them. The pure basalt of the Causeway is said to consist of fifty parts of silicious earth, twenty-five parts of argillaceous and calcareous earth, and twenty-five parts of iron. Iron and flint are therefore its chief component parts; and hence arises the extraordinary weight and closeness of the stone, and the beautiful polish it takes; hence, too, its great fusibility, and the rusty brownish tinge with which its naturally deep black surface is sometimes covered; hence, in fine, arises the phenomenon of all these columns and headlands being magnetic. Flint, as well as iron, having a natural tendency to crystallize in regular forms, it is probable that these two principal constituents of the basalt were pre-eminently active in its formation into regular figures. In general, the grains of the basaltic mass of which the pillars of the Causeway are composed, are very close, compact, and smooth; yet there are sometimes found in it many unfilled spaces, little hollows, air-holes, and fissures. These fissures and holes are usually full of a great variety of crystals,—chalcedony and opal, zeolite, stilibite, natrolite, and sometimes rock crystal. All these are offered to visitors in quantities by the guides, who are constantly collecting them; and amongst these, the zeolites are frequently most beautiful, being usually of a fibrous crystallization, which sends out from a centre elegant, white, glittering hairs of stone, sometimes as fine as the down of a swan's feather. All this it is requisite to know, in order fully to enjoy a visit to the Giant's Causeway, and its neighbourhood, or to reap advantage from perusing a description of it.

The giant who is fabled to have built this Causeway, is Finn Mac-Cul, or Fingal, the Scotch and Irish Hercules. As at one point of the opposite coast of Scotland similar pillars are visible, and were known to the inhabitants of Ireland in times of old, they fabled that Fingal had formed a road from hence to Scotland, but that in more recent times the greatest part of his work sunk into the sea, by which it is now covered. The deep meaning concealed in this fable is, probably, that the basaltic formations in Scotland, as well as those in Ireland, were produced by one and the same natural cause, and thus are nearly connected. Even the basalt cape on the island of Staffa was probably produced at the same time, by the same occurrence; as the inhabitants there also ascribe the basaltic pillars to the same Fingal, and call the cave formed by them Fingal's Cave. It is also not unlikely that the basalt connecting these three points is continued beneath the sea, and that the bottom of the ocean is, as the people say, actually paved with pillars.

———

All this is very grand and poetical in the popular legend; but they were not content with this, and have gone so far as to seek out for the giant all kinds of domestic conveniences, and have discovered the Giant's Loom, the Giant's Chair, the Giant's Theatre, the Giant's Gateway, the Giant's Well, the Giant's Organ, and the Giant's Honeycomb. However far-fetched may be the resemblance with the aforesaid things, every portion has now at least its name, and can therefore be easily described.

The Giant's Well is a little spring, which issues from between some pillars on the western side of the Causeway, and runs down over the cliff into the sea. The Honeycomb and the Organ are the most remarkable of the giant's other utensils. The Organ is not a part of the Causeway itself, but is situated at one side, on the mountain, and consists of a number of large pillars, which grow smaller towards both sides, like the strings of a harp, and is completely apart from the other colonnade, so that one may easily imagine a giant organist sitting before it, particularly since the columns, when struck, actually send forth a metallic ring. Could we discover means for striking them with sufficient force, we might doubtless play on them as on a dulcimer. The Honeycomb is an assemblage of projecting pillars, which stand in the middle of the Causeway; and not far from it is the Giant's Loom, which contains the tallest pillars here exposed to the light of day, being about thirty-three feet high. This middle portion is called the Middle Causeway; while on the right is a Great, and on the left a Little, Giant's Causeway. The most extreme end of the Great Causeway projects, when the water is smooth, 700 feet into the sea, before it is covered by it. When the sea is stormy, and the waves are thrown up very high, the entire length of the Causeway is seen only at momentary intervals. This was the case when I was there, and was, I believe, the reason why I could not rightly distinguish the three divisions of the Causeway.

Another, and at present actually existing, giant, has, in addition to all the gigantic matters already mentioned, arranged a sort of cabinet or saloon, and furnished it with benches. This is Lord Antrim, who, as the present lord and master of this stupendous work of nature, and of many other marvels besides, may well be called a giant. It would be no easy task to describe all the wonders which this nobleman calls his own. His lordship, of whom the poor people in the neighbourhood always speak as their fore-fathers probably did of Fingal, has, on the western part of the Causeway, formed a recess, open on one side towards the sea, and sheltered on the other three by breaking away several rows of columns, so that their stumps, which remain standing around, form a kind of divan. This the people call 'My Lord's Parlour.' Here his lordship, on hunting parties and other occasions, has given some little entertainments. The greatest festival, however, which is repeated every year at the Giant's Causeway, and brings together a vast crowd, and produces the merriest scenes, is a fair, which is held here every 13th of August. The whole way from the inn to the coast is then covered with tents, and if the weather is calm, they extend to the tops of the pillars of the Causeway itself. It must be an interesting spectacle to see the motley wares of an Irish fair amid these black and gigantic works of nature.

The guides on the Causeway are particularly zealous in pointing out to the traveller all the pillars which are remarkable either for their extraordinary size, their height, or the number of their sides. First, there are some perfectly square, with all their sides and angles equal; then hexagonal ones, mathematically equilateral and equiangular; then a triangular one; and, lastly, an eight-sided, and a nine-sided pillar. The triangular column is said to be the only one of its kind on the whole Giant's Causeway. The octagonal one they showed me, and which is called the 'Keystone,' is surrounded by eight hexagonal pillars. The nine-sided one is also said to be unique at the Causeway: Hamilton, it is true, says that there are three such pillars; but my twenty guides all protested against it, with the exception of one, who could not, however, prove his case, as we could not resolve to admit that the figures he showed us had nine sides. This is often by no means easy to decide. The nine-sided pillar we saw seemed to be composed of two pillars melted together, for it had one re-entrant angle, and was surrounded by eight other columns. Among 100 pillars, there are supposed to be seventy hexagonal ones, twenty-nine to have five or seven sides, and one to be three, four, eight, or nine-sided. As I have said, it is with difficulty I could tear myself away from the wonders of the Giant's Causeway, and I would fain have carried away in my pocket a specimen of every species of pillar, or at least have made and taken with me an accurate model of it in wood or stone; but if the philosopher has reason to exclaim *Ars longa, vita brevis*[1], the traveller may as justly complain that the day is too short for the many beauties he has to visit.

---

[1] 'Art is long, life is brief'

The Bays and Headlands

Almost still more beautiful, and nearly as interesting, are the bays and headlands in the neighbourhood of the Causeway. Along the entire coast, from the mouth of the little river Bush to the far-projecting promontory of Bengore, is a succession of little, deep, elegant, round bays. These bays are all surrounded with lofty basaltic shores, with a double row of columns, with strata of ochre, sandstone, and clay-slate, so that each resembles an amphitheatre. The headlands, lofty and rugged, (each of which has, at the base of its extremity, either a kind of little Causeway, or a multitude of great basalt boulder-stones, or some basalt rocks, which look like ruins or tall chimneys,) form a close succession of magnificent capes, which, in variety or elegance of form, can scarcely be equalled any where else. Viewed from the sea, all these various black headlands seem like a single, dark, lofty mass; and the entire line of coast, for about four miles, is called by the sailors Bengore, that is, the Goat's Head, or the Goat's Mountain. To the traveller on the shore, who can perceive its various little portions, each of them appears majestic and grand enough.

The first bay, which lies on the western side of the Causeway, is called Port Noffer Bay, probably an old Irish name corrupted by the English. A narrow footpath, called the 'Shepherd's Path,' leads up the rugged steep to the highest pinnacle of the cliff, which, as well on its edge as far into the country, is perfectly level and covered with a short grass. On this beautiful level sward one can walk round the curves of the bays, and out even to the extreme points of the headlands; for terrible as the precipices, chasms, rents, and cliffs look from below, they appear quite harmless from above, and at a hundred paces from the edge of the precipice, one has no conception of the wild spectacle, the result of the furious contests of the elements, and of vast volcanic convulsions. The geese and sheep of the neighbouring huts seek their food even on the extreme projecting points of the basalt. Like the sheep, my twenty ragged ciceroni scrambled up the steep, chattering, screaming, one laden with my cloak, another with my umbrella, a third with my telescope, all which they had taken away from me

118

against my will, like so many highwaymen. The wind blew bravely, and their rags fluttered right and left, and thus we sailed up the mountain.

Port Noffer Bay is followed by another, and then another and another. The first is called the Giant's Amphitheatre, at least by my guides; the second Port Keostan, the third Roveran Valley, and, finally, the fourth, Port-na-Spagna. The lofty capes which run out between them, and are 400 feet high, have all separate names. Thus, for instance, they call one 'The Grand View,' another 'Roveran Valley Head,' &c. It was absolutely impossible not to look down into every bay, not to run out on every headland, for the prospects were always surprising, charming, beautiful, and interesting. The high surf, dashing against the points—the smooth waters in the bays—the little islands in their centres—the beautiful roundly-formed shores—the extensive prospect over the wide ocean at their feet—the long coast, as far as Innishowen Head—the narrow entrance to Lough Foyle in the distance,—with beholding this over and over again, one can never be satisfied in the few brief moments of half a day.

The bay called the Giant's Amphitheatre is the most perfect amphitheatre in the universe, not even excepting the world-famous one at Rome. It forms a half-circle, as perfect as any architect could make it, and the rocks slope down towards the centre at the same angle on every side. The steps of the round wall of rock are equally regular: first, there is a colonnade eighty feet high; then a broad projecting circular bench, for the giants we may imagine to have been the guests of Finn Mac-Cul; then another step, sixty feet high, formed of elegantly arranged pillars, followed by another bench, which runs all round; and so on, down to the bottom. The water is completely enclosed with a wall of black boulder-stones, forming, as it were, the bounds of the arena; and the whole presents a scene in describing which no traveller need fear running into exaggeration, for all the images and expressions he can employ must fall far short of the reality.

The wind was so extremely violent, the ridges of the rocks, so narrow, and the turf so wet and slippery, that we (my head guide and myself) thought the safest way to gain the point was to lie down flat on our faces, and thus to creep out to it. All our twenty adjutants followed our example, and crawled one after another out to the point. Here we lay, wrapped in clothes or in rags as we were, clinging to the grass with our hands and feet, while the storm raged up between the jagged rocks, bringing with it the moist light sea-foam to a height of 400 feet, which alighted on our clothes, and fled landwards, high over our heads. The view from the extremity of the precipice out over the sea, and in towards the basaltic rocks and columns, was so sublime, that I well nigh forgot my corporeal existence, and imagining nymphs and sirens ready to draw me down into the depths below, clung still more tenaciously to the turf, to resist them, as well as the storm and the giddiness that seized my brain. I lay stretched across the lofty embankment, looking down into the western bay, an example which all my Paddies followed, and also looked down into the western bay. I then crept around, brought my head to the eastern side, letting my feet hang down over the western, and was immediately imitated by my Paddies, all of whom gazed down into the eastern bay, while their tattered breeches and naked legs hung dangling over the western side of the precipice. They were always most anxious to tell me something interesting, and kept shouting to each other, in spite of storm and foam. 'This bay, your honour, is called Port-na-Spagna, that is, the Port of Spain; and those black, high rocks, before the point there, are the Chimney-tops. Both, your honour, have received their names from the Spaniards, troth from the great Spanish Armada itself. One of the great, big ships of this armada, your honour, that was to destroy England, was driven from her course by such another storm as is blowing to-day, and separated from the fleet, and driven against Bengore Head. They took these rocks for big chimneys, like those in England now, but which did not exist then, and bombarded them, and battered down some of them, which have ever since been rolling about in the surf. It was not till their ship was shattered to pieces, and the poor fellows taken prisoners, that they found out their mistake.' On the Scottish coast, also, some points are still shown as the scenes of the destruction of ships of that armada; and the admiral's vessel, with Medina Sidonia, it is well known was driven even as far as the Shetland Isles.

We crept safely back again to the above-mentioned goose-pasture, and after crawling round some other remarkable bays and headlands, we at length arrived at Pleaskin Promontory, or as it is properly called in Irish 'Plaisg-cian,' i.e. the dry head. This Pleaskin is the finest of all the headlands, as the Giant's Causeway is the finest of all the bays. Its form is handsome, and of grand dimensions, its imposing mass advancing into the sea in a half-oval shape, like the bastion of a mighty fortress. Its structure is curious and varied, for it presents no less than twelve or thirteen different strata or steps, one over another, among which the grand double colonnade, so often already mentioned, is the most remarkable. Its steep, black strata and steps of basalt, the bright green of its grass-covered summit, and of some patches of herbs or mosses—I could not clearly distinguish which—and, lastly, some dark red streaks and rocks, the ochre-strata saturated with oxide of iron, and consequently red-coloured, are pleasingly contrasted with one another. Hamilton, (who wrote fifty years ago, and whose work, again printed in 1839, is still the source most to be relied on for information concerning the Giant's Causeway, and, generally, for the entire basalt district of the north of Ireland,[1] gives the measures of the strata of which Pleaskin is composed as follows:—

No.		Feet
1	Summit. Thin layer of earth and sward. Irregular basalts, shivered and cracked at the surface	12
2	Perpendicular range of coarse pillars, containing air-holes	60
3	Coarse bed of rude amorphous basalts, showing marks of a tendency toward forms, resembling an imperfect crystallization	60
4	Second range of regular pillars, neat, and divided into joints	40
5	Bed of red argillaceous ochre, on which the second range of pillars rests	
6	A thin course of iron ore amid the bed of ochre	--22
7	Soft argillaceous stone, of various colours, and mottled appearance, friable, and resembling a variety of steatites	
8	Succession of five or six coarse beds of table basalts, between which thin strata of ochre and other substances occur	180
		374

We give our readers this estimate in order to assist their imagination in forming a clear conception of the exterior of this coast. Pleaskin was immediately succeeded by Port-na-Trughen, i.e. the 'Bay of Sighs'. According to the accounts of the people, as well as to the descriptions of

[1] This is any thing but creditable to Irish geologists; for though Mr. Hamilton's is doubtless an excellent work, still the north of Ireland is surely deserving of being again illumined with the torch of the science of our own days, [original footnote].

credible travellers, some long-drawn sounds are produced in the fissures and chasms of the rocks surrounding this bay, which exactly resemble the sighs and tones of complaint of the human voice. I had hoped that I also might hear these mourning notes of nature; but the great long sigh of the storm was too loud, and in its universal noise and roaring all other sighs were drowned. This at least, and the unfavourable direction of the wind, was the reason assigned by my attendants for my not hearing the sighs. Another traveller, who was more fortunate, thus describes these sounds:— 'While I stood contemplating the wild scenery of the bay, I suddenly heard a heavy long-drawn sigh, quite near me as I imagined. Methought the sound was a human one, and yet I was certain that I was entirely alone. In fact, I was frightened for a moment, and listened with a beating heart as the sighs were repeated at regular intervals. On closer examination, I found that the sound proceeded from a fissure of the rock whereon I was standing. But this was not all: At a little distance I discovered a second fissure, from which groans and sighs also issued, and which sometimes resembled the groans of a person lying in the agonies of death, so much so that it was quite painful to listen to. I visited Port-na-Trughen three times, and each time I heard these sounds exactly as I have described them.'

The less I heard these sighs of nature, the more reason I had here at Port-na-Trughen, (whose nomen was for me an omen,) to do all the sighs myself; for it was here that the prematurely sleepy October sun, which had hidden his morose countenance the entire day, treacherously left us completely in the lurch. And two important things were still undone: first, the ascent of the extreme summit of the real Bengore Head; and, secondly, an examination of the ruins of Dunluce Castle, the most interesting on the northern coast of Ireland, which lie about two miles to the west of the Giant's Causeway. Had Apollo given me even the light of a farthing candle, I would certainly have used it to visit Dunluce Castle. But he took all away with him, probably because he had need of it all to rouge his favourite children, the swarthy Aethiopes, and accordingly he left us Europeans buried in night, and mist, and sighs.

Tired and weary, I sat down on the lofty edge of the Bay of Sighs—always, of course, with my twenty guides—and sighed, first to the east, towards Bengore Head. The heads of the old promontories, unshaken after many a storm, stood along the shore like venerable sages, dark Bengore closing the rank. My guides told me—all twenty at once, in unison!—that a pair of eagles dwelt on the top of Bengore, and had built and bred there from time immemorial. At Fair Head, also, I had been told of a similar pair of eagles; thus it appears that these birds every where select only the highest points. My second sigh was directed to the east, to Dunluce Castle, which I had seen beckoning me so near at many points of my coast-expedition, and which was now, alas! separated from me by four miles of volcanic basalt. My sigh was echoed by all my twenty guides, so heartily, that I almost thought it came from a deft in the rock.

'Ah, your honour! you will be sorry your whole life long that you have not seen Dunluce, and that you cannot turn thither to-morrow.' There is not another castle in the world in such an extraordinary situation. The rock is a great cubical block, which has been separated from the shore, and lies surrounded on all sides by wild surf and breakers. On the land side is a cleft, which is crossed by the remains of a wooden bridge. The top of the rock is almost quite level, though the sides are so rugged that a swallow would find it hard to get up them. Its entire summit is covered with ruins, towers, houses, and mason-work, to the very edge, like a beer-glass with froth. Maiva's Tower, Mac Quillan's Tower, the great old castle-wall, all are still to be seen. There are many courts, some inner, some outer, and round them lie the ruins. Some fragments of houses and walls have fallen into the sea, the rock having given way under them, and now lie with the boulder-stones in the surf. Part of the fortification is built on the land side also, and though all lies in ruin, yet the plan may be still distinctly traced; and what renders it particularly handsome is, that a great part of the walls of the castle is built of the natural columns and columnar blocks of basalt, many of which are so placed as to show their polygonal sides plainly on the outside. To the present day, the black basalt is generally used for buildings in the neighbourhood of the coast.

This castle of Dunluce, whose name, though that of a ruin, is still borne by the eldest son of the Earl of Antrim, was in times beyond memory built and inhabited, and was for more than a thousand years, down to the reign of Queen Elizabeth, the seat and fastness of several proud independent races. The law of the strongest, the right of robbery, oppression of vassals, and all its concomitants, were abolished here, on the basalt coast of Ireland, as also in the highland valleys of neighbouring Scotland, later perhaps than in any other part of Europe. I hardly think that we in Germany, so late as Queen Elizabeth's time, had such haughty knights, or castle-lords, or mountain-kings, as was that Mac Donnell of Dunluce, who received the Queen of England's letter-patent so rudely. This queen sent to the said Mac Donnell—his name at full length was Sorley Buye Mac Donnell—as a mark of her favour, a long, handsomely-ornamented epistle, in which all his possessions, castles, and titles were confirmed. Instead of thanking the gracious queen for this, kissing her hand, and submissively mingling with her vassals, Mac Donnell received the letter as an exceeding insult, drew his sword, cut the parchment in pieces, and threw them into the fire of the castle-hall, declaring that he would not be indebted to any sheep's-skin for what he had acquired by his own good sword.

Those Mac Donnells, who are still in possession of Dunluce, and, as I have said, of the best estates in the county of Antrim, belong to the so often named Antrim family, and came over from Scotland in the year 1580. Their predecessors in the possession of Dunluce, and the entire territory adjoining, called the Root, or the Route, were the Mac Quillans or Magwillies, an aboriginal and famous Irish family. With respect to the manner in which the still flourishing Mac Donnells came into possession of their possessions, and how the old kings of the coast, the Mac Quillans, sunk into their present insignificance, there is a very interesting account by Hamilton, taken from an ancient manuscript. As this account, in a short space, throws a very clear light on the ancient history of the country or coast I have described, and may give my readers an idea of the manner in which the old Irish families lost their properties, how such events were brought about, and what English and Scottish families were their successors, I will here give the purport of it, which is the more interesting, as the matters related in it refer to the beginning of the power of the two richest families of the north of Ireland at the present day, namely, the family of the Earls of Antrim (the Mac Donalds as they were then called, the Mac Donnells as they now write their name), and that of the Marquis of Donegal (Chichester), whom I mentioned before at Belfast.

The Irish chieftains, the Mac Quillans, were the original and ancient lords of Dunluce, and rulers of the adjoining territory as far as the river Bann. On the one side they were engaged in continual strife with the neighbouring chieftains beyond the river Bann, while on the other they were exposed to the attacks and forays of the Scottish islanders, who lay to the north-east of them.

In the year 1580 a Mac Donald, as Hamilton writes the name,—though the Antrim family call themselves Mac Donnells—came from Cantire to Ireland, with a parcel of Halanders (highlanders), to assist the chieftain Tyrconnell against the great O'Nial, with whom he was then at war. In passing through the land of the Mac Quillans, he was civilly received and hospitably entertained by the Mac Quillan, who was then lord and master of the Root. Mac Quillan was the more friendly towards Mac Donald, as he happened to be then at war with the men beyond the river Bann; for the custom of this people was, to rob from every one, and the strongest party carried it, be it right or wrong.

On the day when Mac Donald was taking his departure to proceed on his journey to Tyrconnell, Mac Quillan, who was not equal in war to his savage neighbours, called together all his 'Gallogloghs,' as these Irish lords called their militia, vassals, and retainers, to revenge his affronts beyond the Bann; and Mac Donald, thinking it uncivil not to offer his service that day to Mac Quillan, after having been so kindly treated, sent one of his gentlemen with an offer of his service in the field. Mac Quillan was right well pleased with the offer, and declared it to be a perpetual obligation on him and his posterity. So Mac Quillan and the Highlanders went against the enemy, and where there was a cow taken from Mac Quillan's people before, there were two restored back: after which Mac Quillan and the knight Mac Donald returned to Dunluce with a great prey, and without the loss of a man, where they gave themselves up to rejoicings for their victory, and all the pleasure Mac Quillan could command.

Winter then drawing nigh, Mac Quillan, more good-hearted and hospitable than prudent and cunning, gave Mac Donald an invitation to stay with him at his castle, advising him to settle himself until the spring, and to quarter his men up and down the Root. This, Mac Donald, who was pleased with the mode of living at Dunluce, and had also cast an eye on Mac Quillan's daughter, accepted after some pressing. The men were quartered two and two through the Root; that is to say, one of Mac Quillan's Gallogloghs and a Highlander in every tenant's house. 'In the mean time,' says the manuscript, 'Mac Donald seduced Mac Quillan's daughter and privately married her; on which ground the Scots afterwards founded their claim to Mac Quillan's territories.'

While this was going on at Dunluce Castle, the Highlanders and the Gallogloghs were not on the most friendly terms. In the castle, love was the occasion of strife; in the huts it arose, as usual, from the distribution of provisions. It so happened that the Galloglogh, according to custom, besides his ordinary rations, was entitled to a *meather*[1] of milk, as a privilege. This the Highlanders deemed a great affront; and at last one of them asked his host—'Why do you not give me milk as you give to the other?' The Galloglogh, who was sitting by drinking his milk, immediately replied for his host, 'Wouldst thou, Highland beggar as thou art, compare thyself to me, or any of Mac Quillan's Gallogloghs.' The poor honest tenant, who was heartily tired of them both, said, 'Pray, gentlemen, I'll open the two doors, and you may go and fight it out in the fair fields, and he that gets the victory let him take milk and all to himself.' The combat ended in the death of the Galloglogh; 'after which,' as the manuscript says, 'the Highlander came in again and dined heartily.'

The affair of course soon became known, and Mac Quillan's Gallogloghs assembled to demand satisfaction. A council was held, in which the conduct of the Scots, their great and dangerous power in the Root, and the disgrace arising from the seduction of Mac Quillan's daughter, was debated, and it was agreed that each Galloglogh should kill his comrade Highlander by night, and their lord and master with them. But Mac Quillan's daughter, the wife of Mac Donald, discovered the plot, and told it to her husband. As Mac Quillan too, who was by this time tired of his guests, was not a stranger to the conspiracy, Mac Donald took the advice of his friends, and fled with them and his wife in the night-time, and escaped to the island of Raghery, which being at this time (A. D. 1580) uninhabited, they were forced to feed on colts' flesh, for want of other provisions.

From this beginning, the Mac Donalds and the Mac Quillans entered on a war, and continued to worry each other during the reign of Queen Elizabeth, while now the Mac Donalds, and now the Mac Quillans, were lords of Dunluce and of the Root. This war continued till the English power became so superior in Ireland that both parties made an appeal to James I., who had just then ascended the throne of England. This king, as is

---

[1] A vessel commonly used by the old Irish, formed out of one solid piece of wood, and usually of a triangular shape. [original footnote].

well known, had a predilection for his Scotch countrymen. He accordingly made over to the Mac Donald, by letters patent, four great baronies, including, along with other lands, all poor Mac Quillan's possessions. However, to preserve some appearance of justice, he gave to Mac Quillan a grant of the great barony of Ennishowen, the old territory of the O'Doghertys in Donegal, and sent to him Sir John Chichester, to inform him of this decision and to carry it into execution.

Mac Quillan was extremely mortified at his ill success, and very disconsolate at the difficulties which attended the transport of his poor people over the river Bann, and the Lough Foyle, which lay between him and his new territory. The crafty Englishman, taking advantage of his situation, by an offer of some lands which lay nearer his old dominions, persuaded him to cede his title to the remote barony of Ennishowen, in exchange for the district of Clanreaghurkie, which belonged to the Chichesters. The honest and deeply afflicted Mac Quillan and his people settled on this little estate, while the Chichesters took possession of the great barony, which, along with other estates, and the title of Marquis of Donegal, they possess to this day.

Thus the Mac Quillans fell from the fine castle of Dunluce and the Root to a little estate in the interior of the country. But they fell still farther: for one of them, Bury Oge Mac Quillan, who, after the old Irish fashion and the custom of the Mac Quillans, wished to be more hospitable and generous than his scanty income could afford, sold his estate at a low price to the Chichesters, and, instead of a landed property, had now a full purse. This he spent in hospitality and generosity, as long as any thing remained in it; and thus at length fell the old Irish family of the Mac Quillans. At the end of the last century, Mac Quillans were still to be found on the Clanreaghurkie estate, amongst the lowest of the people, in the enjoyment of nothing to distinguish them from the rest of the peasants, except, the title of King Mac Quillan, bestowed on them in mockery by their neighbours. I have already mentioned that in many other parts of Ireland the descendants of such kings are frequently to be found among peasants, stablemen, &c.

Return and Conclusion

Roses and Myrtles Beneath the Snow—Whinstone—Clan's-Names—'The Moss is so Far'—Sea-Plants—Their Use—Their Elegant Forms—Herbarium of Sea-Plants—Return

With this we concluded our sigh about Dunluce, as we sat by the Bay of Sighs. In the mean time it had become perfectly dark, and with some trouble and difficulty I found my way to my car, and returned, late in the evening, to Ballycastle, and found, alas! that the Misses Mac Donnell had also sunk, if not into the lowest rank of their clan, at least into the pillow of their soft couch.

On the following day (the 25th Oct.) I hoped at last for a change of weather; and so, in fact, it happened. The storm, which the day before had been dry, had during the night laden itself with snow, and was busily engaged in powdering the rocks, as I set out in the morning on my return to Belfast. This return journey I had intended to make by Coleraine and Antrim; but thinking that I could hardly find in the interior any thing more interesting than a repetition of the noble coast of Antrim, which besides would present a very different appearance in the snow, I returned by the road I came. The shading of snow was different on every field I passed. On the stubble-fields it had melted less than on the grass; on the moors, more than on the heaths; and the figures of many districts were distinctly to be recognized on the snow-covered surface. I had thus, doubtless, in the snowflakes, a very neat thermometer for the different degrees of warmth of the soil, and the living and dead plants.

It is generally said that the coast of Antrim is so mild, that the snow never remains on the ground, even when, some miles inland, the hills are deeply covered with it. This may be the case; but I have the evidence of my own eyes that it falls at least as early as October on this mild coast. The blooming roses, that showed themselves in great abundance on some farms, glowed like fire from beneath the snow-flakes that hung on them. Yet mild as the climate is, it is in many respects extremely disagreeable to man. How well some plants bear it, is shown by the myrtles of Glenarm, which I visited once more. Those myrtles, like the arbutus of Mount Kennedy, are the most famous and largest of their kind in Ireland. I was informed that a gardener from the Royal Gardens at Kew, once made a pilgrimage in person to see these myrtles, and to examine closely their situation, and the nature of the country around them.

Among other remarkable things in the Castle of Glenarm, besides a model of the Giant's Causeway, I saw also a large piece of Irish rock-crystal, which is found here in the basaltic caves. It was from four and a half to five inches long, and is said to be the largest ever found here. I was also told that the people of the north of Ireland every where call the basalt, 'Whinstone.' I had, indeed, often before heard this word; but I did not know that it was a peculiar North-Irish and Scotch provincialism. 'Whin' is the shrub called furze, so common in Ireland, and which grows in abundance on the basalt rocks. The fair lady who told me this, also informed me, that here, in the north of Ireland, what the English call family names, are often called clans-names by the common people; and that if I wished to get a clear conception of the meaning of the word clan, I had only to think of what is called in the Bible the 'Children of Israel.' For the Irish and Scotch used the word precisely in the same sense, as is proved by their translating the 'Children of Israel,' always by 'Clan Israel.' It is remarkable that every thing here, both in customs and language, even among the native Irish, approaches to the north of England and Scotland. Thus, what in all the rest of Ireland is called 'bog,' the people here term 'moss' as in England and Scotland. 'The moss here is at a great distance,' said the people in Glenarm, when I complained of their putting so little turf on my fire. That the moss or bog is so far off, is the daily complaint of thousands of poor Irish. That they have a moss or a bog near, is the daily joy and happiness of many thousands more. Whether the moss or bog be nearer far off, is a question inquired into and carefully examined in purchases, in taking leases, and on a hundred other occasions.

The storm had thrown up an unusual quantity of seaweed at Glenarm, and different other places along the coast. Half the population were next morning, when the wind had somewhat abated, busy gathering it, and taking it away on little cars. All the wet basalt and limestone rocks, which rolled about on the seashore, were covered with men, women, and children, who, as at a joyful harvest-home, gathered the long snake-like slimy weeds, and collected them all carefully into little heaps. The Irish turn these plants to many uses: in the first place, they eat them, and, indeed, in no small quantities. Several of my twenty guides at the Giant's Causeway amused themselves on the way with chewing different marine plants, just as they picked them out of the surf. I saw the people in Ballycastle, too, putting seaweed on their bread and butter, and eating it as we do water cresses. In Belfast, I saw the peasants bring sea-plants to market as a common vegetable, just as they do peas or beans in our country. Some seaweed they salt and boil, and then it has exactly the same appearance as our German plum jam. One may call those boiled seaweeds, Irish jam. Besides, as I have already said, they make kelp from the ashes of the burnt sea-plants, both in Ireland and Scotland; and those which they neither eat nor burn for kelp, they use as manure. Yet I believe they are not here so often used for the latter purpose as on our Baltic coasts, the sandy shores of which gain more benefit from this kind of manure than the wet morass lands of Ireland, which would be more benefitted by lime, sea-sand, and shells, which latter are here and there on the coast of Ireland, at Lough Foyle, for instance, piled up in large heaps, even in entire hills.

All the coasts of Ireland are very rich in various kinds of sea-plants, and accordingly it seems that the green vegetation of the Emerald Isle is continued even beneath the sea. The coasts of Antrim are said to be the richest of all the coasts of Ireland, in those plants, which grow and spread more quickly on limestone and basalt than on other kinds of stone. Those sea-plants which the Irish consider edible, are pretty numerous. The following are some of the most esteemed:—Above all, the Dillisk (Rhodominia palmata); then the kind they call Murlius (Laminaria saccharina); and, lastly, the Carrigeen Moss (Chondrus erispus). This latter kind they dry in the sun, and use as a substitute for Iceland moss. Hence it is generally termed 'Irish Moss.' At Belfast, and on the sea-coast, a pound of dillisk often costs no more than a penny; while in the interior of the country it costs threepence or fourpence. They often praise highly its fine taste and flavour, and sharply criticise the bad qualities of the inferior kinds of dulse, as dillisk is frequently called; whilst to one who is not experienced in those niceties of taste, both the delicate and spoiled kinds are equally nauseous. In some places on the coast of Antrim, as well as in some coast districts of Scotland, the people are so much in the habit of eating various kinds of seaweed, that they never cease chewing it, and always carry some dulse or dillisk about with them, as the common people in Germany do tobacco. The sea-plant which they cook is called Sloke, Slokaun, or Laver (Porphyra laciniata). It is generally collected during the autumn and winter, as in summer it is too tough. After being washed and cleansed, this laver is boiled with butter, and then sold in tin measures: it is eaten with pepper and vinegar, and is sent in barrels even to London.

For manure, a kind which is distinguished by the name of 'sea-wrack,' is principally used. This is the Laminaria digitata, which is so good a manure, especially for potatoes, that it is proverbially said here, on the coast of Antrim, 'a sack of sea-wrack will produce a sack of potatoes.' It is, however, in quantity rather than in quality that the potatoes are improved by it. After every storm, the coast of Antrim is crowded like a fair, and all the people come down from their hills to gather sea-wrack for their potatoes. When the sea is perfectly calm, they wade as far into the water as they can, and cut away the weeds under the water with sickles. What does not the poor Irishman do to get a few "tatoes!' They take with them their little mountain horses, and load the manure on their backs; or, if the ground is too rocky for horses, they load their own backs with the briny, dripping manure.

From the difficulty of observing them beneath the water, where alone they unfold all their splendour, very few know the delicacy, and uncommon beauty and elegance of form, assumed by these products of marine vegetation, which are scarcely inferior in any respect to those of our gardens. When drawn out, they have commonly a very melancholy appearance, on account of the mud and water with which they are covered. Nothing but drying and unfolding them in an artist-like manner can restore them in some degree to their natural state. While all other flowers and plants lose by drying and preserving in the herbarium, sea-plants are the only ones which gain in the process; and a careful drying is the only means of enabling their beauty to be observed and enjoyed by the lovers of nature. Dr. Drummond, of Belfast, has written a very learned little treatise on the drying of those plants, of which he has a beautiful and perfect collection.

It is inexplicable that the importance of this art is not more perceived, and that all museums do not contain herbaries of these wonderful little plants which the sea conceals. If museums are intended for the use of the lover of nature, and in particular to furnish him with knowledge and instruction in matters which would be otherwise inaccessible, then a herbary of sea-plants is infinitely more pressingly necessary in every museum than a herbary of land-plants. The latter, showing but imperfectly the forms of nature, can add but little to her glory; but a herbarium of marine plants is absolutely an elevating and beautifying of the works of creation, and adds to the glory of the Creator. Dr. Drummond also remarks, in the treatise I have mentioned, that one description of seaweed (Polysiphonia violacea), which has very long black stalks, when it is driven about by the waves in a storm in great quantities on the coast of Antrim, entangles and felts itself with its long branches so as to accumulate in large lumps, which roll about on the shore, and often form knots so firm that it is almost impossible to unloose them.

I drank another glass of whisky in Glenarm—the mild climate of Ireland soon teaches one whisky drinking—for my car-driver told me it was the last good whisky we could procure on the coast,—the Larne whisky was no good, and the Carrickfergus whisky was still worse. We then proceeded towards Belfast. I felt myself exceedingly comfortable on one side of my body, which, in one corner of my car, was sheltered from the attack of the snow and wind, and I did all in my power to concentrate all my sense of feeling and my whole soul into this comfortable corner, and to let all my other limbs freeze and shiver in the wet and cold as much as they pleased. Most people say that if one part of the body, the feet, for instance, or the head, is cold, one feels uncomfortable all over, however warm the rest of him may be; but I think my theory is better, and that one may bring himself, with some persuasion and management, to feel contented and warm if but one limb be well off. I occupied my thoughts with this theory till I arrived at Belfast, where I had an opportunity of drying my papers and clothes one by one.

And when I had effected this, I took my leave of Erin, and embarked for Caledonia.

The End of "Travels In Ireland".

Index

134

Clachan Publishing Travel books

Antiquarian republications

Travels In Ireland - *J.G. Kohl* - This is a very readable account by a German visitor of his tour around Ireland immediately before the Great Famine. (1845).

J.G.Kohl's account has been sub-divided for the convenience of local and family historians.

- **Travels in Ireland – Part 1,** takes us through Edgeworthtown, The Shannon, Limerick, Edenvale, Kilrush and Father Mathew.
- **Travels in Ireland – Part 2,** his journey continues through Tarbet, Tralee, Killarney, Bantry, Cork, Kilkenny and Waterford.
- **Travels in Ireland – Part 3,** this section deals with Wexford, Enniscorthy, Avoca, Glendalough and Dublin.
- **Travels In Ireland - Part 4 –** he goes north for the last part of his journey through Dundalk, Newry, Belfast, The Antrim Coast, Rathlin, The Giant's Causeway.

A Journey throughout Ireland, During the Spring, Summer and Autumn of 1834 - *Henry D. Inglis* - Inglis travels Ireland attempting to answer the question, 'is Ireland and improving country?' using discussion with landlords, manufacturers and tenants plus his own insightful observations.

Henry D. Inglis' account has also been sub-divided for the convenience of local and family historians.

- **A Journey throughout Ireland, During the Spring, Summer and Autumn of 1834, Part 1** takes us from Dublin. Through Wexford, Waterford and Cork.
- **A Journey throughout Ireland, During the Spring, Summer and Autumn of 1834, Part 2** is an account of Kerry, Clare, Limerick and the Shannon and concludes in Athlone.

Highways and Byways in Donegal and Antrim - *Stephen Gwynn* - Take this book with you as you travel around Donegal and the Glens of Antrim and you will find that you journey not only over land, but also over time, (1901).

Stephen Gwynn's account has also been sub-divided for the convenience of local and family historians.

- **Highways and Byways in Donegal and Antrim Part One: Donegal**
- **Highways and Byways in Donegal and Antrim Part: Two - Derry & Co. Antrim.**

Recent travel books

Valhalla and the Fjörd: A Spiritual Motorcycle Journey through the History of Strangford Lough - *Peter Moore* - As former Director of archaeological excavations, the author has researched the sites and monuments with professional care, going beyond archaeology , the spirituality and aura the sites exude.

Ulster and the City of Belfast - *Richard Hayward* - This is Hayward's most significant piece of travel writing and is republished in response to the considerable interest in Hayward on the 50th anniversary of his death. This quality paperback edition has a new foreword by Paul Clements and includes all Raymond Piper's original illustrations

Aghaidh Achadh Mór, The Face of Aghamore – edited by Joe Byrne. This is a reproduction of a title originally published in 1991 and is of enduring interest to local historians and to those with ancestral roots in East Mayo. It covers such topics as Stone Age archaeology, family history, local hedge schools, O'Carolan's connection with the parish, the Civil War and townland surveys.

Ballads and Songs

Songs of the Glens of Antrim, Moiré O'Neill

These Songs of the Glens of Antrim were written by a Glenswoman in the dialect of the Glens, and chiefly for the pleasure of other Glens-people.

Away with Words - by Michael Sands

A book of poems of family, home, place and music in North Antrim.

"What a joy it has been to have discovered this marvellous collection. It represents a bright shaft of welcome sunlight in a wearying world. It is full of joy, hope, intellect and a deep understanding of who we are and the unquestioned importance of hearth, home and music." - Mickey MacConnell,- songwriter and journalist

A Moment's Notice

by Michael Sands - *"This collection, Michael's second, is rooted in his environment: family, society, music, the natural world outside his window. The poems keenly observe the everyday, drawing our attention to its finer details, which are presented to us with fondness and irreverent mirth. Michael's poetry at times sparkles with wit and clever rhymes, and at others it is earnest in its tenderness and humanity. Underlying the verse is an encompassing love for his world and its people – turn the page, and step inside."* - Jason O'Rourke – writer and musician

Clachan
Publishing

Clachan Publishing, Ballycastle, Glens of Antrim.

www.ingramcontent.com/pod-product-compliance
Lightning Source LLC
LaVergne TN
LVHW021504080426
835509LV00018B/2392